I0600799

Cyberwarfare

Peggy J. Parks

The Internet

ReferencePoint
Press®

San Diego, CA

ReferencePoint Press®

About the Author

Peggy J. Parks holds a bachelor of science degree from Aquinas College in Grand Rapids, Michigan, where she graduated magna cum laude. An author who has written over 100 educational books for children and young adults, Parks lives in Muskegon, Michigan, a town that she says inspires her writing because of its location on the shores of Lake Michigan.

© 2013 ReferencePoint Press, Inc.
Printed in the United States

For more information, contact:
ReferencePoint Press, Inc.
PO Box 27779
San Diego, CA 92198
www.ReferencePointPress.com

Picture credits:
Cover: Thinkstock/iStockphoto
AP Images: 12, 16
Steve Zmina: 32–33, 47–49, 62–64, 76–78

LIBRARY OF CONGRESS CATALOGING-IN-PUBLICATION DATA

Parks, Peggy J., 1951–
    Cyberwarfare / by Peggy J. Parks.
        p. cm. -- (Compact research)
    Includes bibliographical references and index.
    ISBN 978-1-60152-264-1 (hbk.) -- ISBN 1-60152-264-9 (hbk.)
    1. Information warfare--Juvenile literature. 2. Cyberterrorism--Juvenile literature 3. Computer security--Juvenile literature. 4. National security--Juvenile literature. I. Title.
    U163.P366   2013
    355.4--dc23
                                                            2012020131

Contents

Foreword

66Where is the knowledge we have lost in information?99

—T.S. Eliot, "The Rock."

As modern civilization continues to evolve, its ability to create, store, distribute, and access information expands exponentially. The explosion of information from all media continues to increase at a phenomenal rate. By 2020 some experts predict the worldwide information base will double every seventy-three days. While access to diverse sources of information and perspectives is paramount to any democratic society, information alone cannot help people gain knowledge and understanding. Information must be organized and presented clearly and succinctly in order to be understood. The challenge in the digital age becomes not the creation of information, but how best to sort, organize, enhance, and present information.

ReferencePoint Press developed the *Compact Research* series with this challenge of the information age in mind. More than any other subject area today, researching current issues can yield vast, diverse, and unqualified information that can be intimidating and overwhelming for even the most advanced and motivated researcher. The *Compact Research* series offers a compact, relevant, intelligent, and conveniently organized collection of information covering a variety of current topics ranging from illegal immigration and deforestation to diseases such as anorexia and meningitis.

The series focuses on three types of information: objective single-author narratives, opinion-based primary source quotations, and facts and statistics. The clearly written objective narratives provide context and reliable background information. Primary source quotes are carefully selected and cited, exposing the reader to differing points of view, and facts and statistics sections aid the reader in evaluating perspectives. Presenting these key types of information creates a richer, more balanced learning experience.

For better understanding and convenience, the series enhances information by organizing it into narrower topics and adding design features that make it easy for a reader to identify desired content. For example, in *Compact Research: Illegal Immigration*, a chapter covering the economic impact of illegal immigration has an objective narrative explaining the various ways the economy is impacted, a balanced section of numerous primary source quotes on the topic, followed by facts and full-color illustrations to encourage evaluation of contrasting perspectives.

The ancient Roman philosopher Lucius Annaeus Seneca wrote, "It is quality rather than quantity that matters." More than just a collection of content, the *Compact Research* series is simply committed to creating, finding, organizing, and presenting the most relevant and appropriate amount of information on a current topic in a user-friendly style that invites, intrigues, and fosters understanding.

Cyberwarfare at a Glance

What Cyberwarfare Is

Cyberwarfare involves deliberate cyberattacks by one or more nations against another; beyond that, government officials, military leaders, and security experts often disagree about what sorts of cybercrimes should be considered acts of cyberwar.

Weapons Used in Cyberwarfare

Two of the most threatening cyberweapons are botnets, an illicit network formed by thousands of hijacked "zombie" computers; and exploits, which take advantage of software flaws.

Cyber Superweapon

The Stuxnet worm is known as a cyber superweapon because it is the first malware designed to destroy real-world machinery.

High-Tech Spying

Cyberespionage involves unauthorized entry into computer systems to copy sensitive and classified information.

Critical Infrastructures

Critical infrastructure industries include banking and finance, public health, information technology, transportation, nuclear power, and utilities such as electricity, oil and gas, and water. Security experts say these industries are vulnerable and a prime target for cyberattackers.

Cyberattackers

With most cyberattacks, the perpetrators are unknown; the United States considers China and Russia to be the leading cyberwarfare adversaries.

Cyberwarfare Threat

Many cybersecurity experts warn that cyberwarfare is an imminent threat and that it is only a matter of time before a massive cyberattack occurs; others insist that the threat is overblown.

Protection Against Cyberattack

Experts who warn about cyberwarfare say that the most crucial steps are acknowledging the threat and tightening computer system security.

Legislation

Proposed laws would make information sharing easier between the government and Internet service providers and strengthen the Department of Homeland Security's authority to regulate security for critical infrastructure industries. Both laws have supporters and opponents.

Retaliation

Using military force against perceived cyberattackers is highly controversial; their identities are often unknown, so hitting the wrong target is likely; also, retaliation could lead to international tension and animosity among countries ostensibly at peace with each other.

Overview

❝The cyber domain is today's equivalent of the untamed American West during the 1800s. Keyboards have replaced revolvers and hackers are the new gunslingers.❞

—Jeffrey Carr, a cyberintelligence expert specializing in the investigation of cyberattacks against governments and infrastructures and the author of *Inside Cyber Warfare: Mapping the Cyber Underworld*.

❝Pure cyber war—'keyboard versus keyboard' or 'geek versus geek'—is unlikely.❞

—James Andrew Lewis, director of the Center for Strategic and International Studies Technology and Public Policy program.

In 2010, when security experts began to scrutinize a computer worm called Stuxnet, they knew it was no ordinary malicious software (malware)—this was a cyber superweapon with the power to destroy real-world machinery. Stuxnet had caught their attention after an incident occurred at a nuclear facility in central Iran. Machines known as centrifuges, which enrich uranium for nuclear power or weapons, were failing one after another: In just six months, at least one thousand centrifuges had inexplicably begun spinning so fast that they flew apart. This happened because Stuxnet had been programmed for a very specific purpose: to crawl through a facility's computer system in search of a piece of equipment known as a programmable logic controller (PLC) and then infect it. German security expert Ralph Langner calls Stuxnet "a carefully constructed weapon designed to . . . infect the system, disguise its presence, move through the network, changing computer code and subtly alter the speed of the centrifuges without the Iranians ever noticing. Sabotage by software."[1]

Because PLCs play a critical role in plant operations for everything from oil and gas pipelines to water treatment facilities, electric companies, nuclear power plants, and even traffic lights, Stuxnet is viewed by security experts as a new generation of malware—one with extraordinary potential for destruction. Says US Air Force officer and cyberweapons expert Robert M. Lee: "Stuxnet has caused a paradigm shift in cyber warfare and changed the way nations, corporations and we as citizens view cyber warfare. This is just the beginning of a new era of warfare that will only become more invasive and costly to each of us."[2]

From Fantasy to a Virtual War Zone

Understanding the concept of cyberwarfare begins with knowing what cyberspace is—and its original meaning was a product of science fiction. Coined by "cyberpunk" author William Gibson, the word *cyberspace* made its debut in a 1982 short story called *Burning Chrome* and was further popularized in the futuristic novel *Neuromancer*. Based solely on what he imagined, Gibson wove intricate tales of cyberspace, an ultrarealistic virtual world of interconnected data.

Although it was conceived as fantasy, cyberspace is now reality. It refers to the state of interconnectedness among human beings, without regard to their location, made possible by computer technology and the Internet. In their book *Cyber War: The Next Threat to National Security and What to Do About It*, cybersecurity experts Richard A. Clarke and Robert K. Knake write: "Cyberspace. . . . It's the laptop you or your kid carries to school, the desktop computer at work. It's a drab windowless building downtown and a pipe under the street. It's everywhere, everywhere there's a com-

> " Although it was conceived as fantasy, cyberspace is now reality. It refers to the state of interconnectedness among human beings, without regard to their location, made possible by computer technology and the Internet. "

puter, or a processor, or a cable connecting to one." Clarke and Knake go on to say that cyberspace has become a much different realm than it was in the past: "Now it's a war zone, where many of the decisive battles in the twenty-first century will play out."[3]

What Is Cyberwarfare?

Throughout history the meaning of war has been clear: enemies fighting to conquer each other using weapons that have grown increasingly sophisticated over time. Enemy nations are still engaged in wars today, but another kind of war is also in progress—cyberwar, in which the weapon is technology. Although cyberwarfare involves serious attacks on computer systems, its meaning has not been well defined. In fact, few people agree about what it means, including government officials, policy makers, military leaders, and security experts. Says internationally renowned security technologist Bruce Schneier: "We don't have good definitions of what cyber war is, what it looks like and how to fight it."[4]

Much of the controversy over cyberwarfare relates to how serious a cyberattack needs to be before it is considered an act of war. Clarke, who served three US presidents as a counterterrorism adviser and then founded his own cybersecurity firm, believes that this pertains to any attempt by a nation-state to cause damage or disruption by penetrating another country's computer systems. Other experts refute Clarke's viewpoint, saying it is far too broad. Says James Andrew Lewis, the director of technology and public policy at the Center for Strategic and International Studies (CSIS) in Washington, DC: "Cyberwar has to meet the same threshold we'd hold any other war to. . . . There has to be physical destruction, and there have to be casualties. If there aren't, it isn't an attack, and it isn't war."[5]

Cyberweaponry

In the same way that soldiers fighting a war depend on guns and bombs to defeat their enemies, malicious hackers rely on cyberweapons that can manipulate and/or destroy computer systems. A number of cyberweapons are known to exist, with botnets (or bots) among the most threatening. Botnets are created when tens or even hundreds of thousands of computers are infected with malware and then hijacked to form an illicit network. This network of "zombie" computers is then controlled and given collective orders by users in remote locations. Says Paul Rosenzweig, who served with the Department of Homeland Security (DHS) and authored the book *Cyberwarfare: How Conflicts in Cyberspace Are Challenging America and Changing the World*: "Once created, botnets are valuable tools for criminal enterprise. But botnets can also be weapons of war—working together, they can crack codes and passwords and attack critical infrastructure systems, like the banking system or the electric grid."[6]

Another type of cyberweapon is the exploit, whose purpose is to take advantage of software flaws. When hackers know about a bug in a computer program, they can "exploit" it by breaking into the code and inserting a virus, worm, or other destructive malware. By far, the most coveted exploits among hackers with criminal intent are zero-day exploits, which utilize software flaws, undiscovered by anyone else, to carry out an attack. Security expert Tony Bradley writes: "The Holy Grail for malicious program and virus writers is the 'zero day exploit.' . . . By creating a virus or worm that takes advantage of a vulnerability the vendor is not yet aware of and for which there is not currently a patch available the attacker can wreak maximum havoc."[7]

> " Much of the controversy over cyberwarfare relates to how serious a cyberattack needs to be before it is considered an act of war. "

Spying, Stealing, and Threatening

Cyberespionage (high-tech spying) is the unauthorized entry into a computer system for the purpose of copying sensitive information such as classified military secrets. Although it is known to be a widespread, threatening problem, whether cyberespionage is a form of cyberwarfare is often debated. For those who say it is not, cyber intelligence expert Jeffrey Carr offers some food for thought: "While espionage between nation states has never been considered grounds for going to war, it has also never occurred at this scale. And if a country's national objectives of accumulating power, influence, and resources can be done virtually instead of on the battlefield, then should cyber espionage be considered a new type of warfare?" Carr presents this rhetorical question to illustrate one example of a serious cyberattack "that may or may not be considered cyberwar."[8]

Security analysts at the US Department of Homeland Security's secretive cyberdefense lab in Idaho monitor cyberspace activity as part of efforts to protect the nation's electrical power grid, water, and communications systems from cyberattacks.

Another high-tech crime that some consider part of cyberwarfare is cyberextortion, which involves threatening governments, companies, or groups, to force them to pay money. This is a growing problem worldwide, which became clear in a 2011 report by the security company McAfee and the CSIS. The report was based on a survey of two hundred executives from fourteen countries who were all affiliated with industries such as energy, oil and gas, and water. One finding was that over the previous two years, 25 percent of respondents had fallen victim to cyberextortion through attack or threat of attack. The report states: "The threat of cyberextortion is widely acknowledged and has been rapidly increasing. . . . Extortion cases are equally distributed among the different sectors of critical infrastructure, signaling no one industry is immune to the reach of these cybercriminals."[9]

The Backbone of Society

When security experts warn about the threats posed by cyberwarfare, one of their top concerns is the vulnerability of critical infrastructures. A wide variety of industries comprise America's infrastructure, including banking and finance, public health, information technology, manufacturing, chemicals, emergency services, energy, water, transportation, and nuclear power. According to the Department of Homeland Security, critical infrastructures are so vital to the United States that if they were incapacitated or destroyed, the effect on national security, the economy, and the health and safety of the population would be disastrous.

All executives involved in the 2011 McAfee/CSIS study were from infrastructure industries—and what they had to say was a wake-up call for cybersecurity experts and government officials. The participants spoke candidly about the acceleration of threats to their computer systems, with nearly two-thirds reporting that they found malware designed for sabotage on a regular basis. The most serious problems were in the utility industries, with some electric companies experiencing thousands of probes (unauthorized attempts to get information) every month. The authors of the report write: "Whether it is cybercriminals engaged in theft or extortion, or foreign governments preparing sophisticated exploits like Stuxnet, cyberattackers have targeted critical infrastructure."[10]

> " According to the Department of Homeland Security, critical infrastructures are so vital to the United States that if they were incapacitated or destroyed, the effect on national security, the economy, and the health and safety of the population would be disastrous. "

Cyberspace Terrorism

Terrorists are extremists—people who have no qualms about committing violent acts in order to get a message across, to intimidate, to punish perceived wrongdoings, and/or to coerce nations or groups into doing what the terrorists want. The same definition applies to cyberterrorists, but their malevolent acts are carried out via computers and the Internet. Retired Federal Bureau of Investigation (FBI) agent and computer security expert William L. Tafoya defines cyberterrorism as, "the intimidation of civilian enterprise through the use of high technology to bring about political, religious, or ideological aims, actions that result in disabling or deleting critical infrastructure data or information."[11]

No one disputes that terrorism is a threat to national security, especially after the devastating September 11, 2001, attacks on the World Trade Center and the Pentagon. But not all security experts believe that terrorists have the capability to plan and launch a major cyberattack. In a March 2011 report for the Congressional Research Service, security experts Catherine A. Theohary and John Rollins write:

> To some observers, the term "cyberterrorism" is inappropriate, because a widespread cyberattack may simply produce annoyances, not terror, as would a bomb, or other chemical, biological, radiological, or nuclear explosive . . . weapon. However, others believe that the effects of a widespread computer network attack would be unpredictable and might cause enough economic disruption, fear, and civilian deaths to qualify as terrorism.[12]

Unknown Enemies

In a physical war those who are fighting know exactly who their enemies are, but the same is not true of cyberwarfare. After an attack has been launched, even top cybersecurity gurus may have no idea which individuals, groups, or countries were responsible for it. This was the case with Stuxnet; since it was discovered in 2010, experts have laboriously combed through the programming code but can still only make educated guesses about who created it. Lee writes: "At this point, attributing Stuxnet to any group of nation-states or corporations would be an ill-advised move, given the known evidence. This is because it is easy to leave false evidence behind in cyberspace."[13]

As with Stuxnet's developers, the perpetrators of a cyberattack on South Korea in March 2011 also remain a mystery. It was a distributed denial of service attack (DDoS), meaning one in which multiple computers infected by the same malware try to access targeted websites simultaneously. This avalanche of traffic bombards the sites and causes servers to crash, which is what happened in South Korea. Numerous websites were disabled in the attack, including those of the Financial Services Commission, defense ministry, National Assembly, military headquarters, US Forces in Korea, and other government agencies. Upon investigation, McAfee researchers found a sophisticated computer worm that was being commanded by servers in multiple countries, including the United States, Taiwan, Saudi Arabia, Russia, India, South Africa, Thailand, Hong Kong, and Australia. Although North Korea was considered the prime suspect, no one knows for sure which country or group was responsible for the attack.

> " In a physical war those who are fighting know exactly who their enemies are, but the same is not true of cyberwarfare. "

How Great a Threat Is Cyberwarfare?

With the continued escalation of cyberattacks, controversy over how threatening cyberwarfare is has grown as well. Experts on one side of the debate, often called cyberhawks or "Cassandras" (people who always predict disaster), warn that it is only a matter of time before a massive cyberattack kicks off a full-scale cyberwar. Others refute that claim, arguing that the threat is grossly overexaggerated. The latter is the viewpoint of Jerry Brito, who directs the Technology Policy Program at George Mason University. Although he does not discount the seriousness of cyberattacks, Brito believes that the threat of cyberwar is being blown out of proportion. "People should worry about this, and take serious action," he says, "but they shouldn't worry about some of these doomsday scenarios. They shouldn't worry about some sort of cyber Pearl Harbor, with planes falling out of the sky and power plants going down all in the span of fifteen minutes."[14]

Many security experts could not disagree more, saying that cyberwar is a looming threat that should not be dismissed or minimized. Says Ta-

North Korea, a prime suspect in a 2011 cyberattack against South Korea, was also implicated in a 2009 attack that overwhelmed computers at US and South Korean government agencies for days. Targets of that attack included the White House, the Pentagon, and the New York Stock Exchange (pictured).

foya: "If people wait until they have absolute proof positive, it may be too late. The cyber trends seem clear. Over the course of approximately 13 years, both the number and frequency of instances of digital disorder have intensified, and the sophistication and diversity of types of cyber attacks have increased."[15] Evidence of Tafoya's claim was revealed in a study by the DHS. The agency discovered that between October 2011 and February 2012, there were eighty-six attacks on US computer systems that control critical infrastructures, factories, and databases—a huge increase over the previous year when eleven attacks were reported.

Vulnerabilities Versus Preparedness

Many security experts warn that the spike in cyberattacks on critical infrastructure industries is a red flag that they are a prime target. In the 2011 McAfee/CSIS study, 40 percent of respondents said their industry's security measures were not keeping pace with escalating threats. When asked how prepared their companies were for malware infestation and/ or DDoS attacks, up to one-third said they were either not very prepared or completely unprepared. The executives were candid about how this worried them, and according to security expert Steve Santorelli, they need to be listened to. "You have to remember that these 200 people who were surveyed really know their stuff," he says. "And if they're scared, then maybe we ought to be as well."[16]

> **In order to thwart cyber-attacks, security experts widely agree that computer system security must be a top priority—but study after study shows that this is rarely the case.**

In order to thwart cyberattacks, security experts widely agree that computer system security must be a top priority— but study after study shows that this is rarely the case. Most critical infrastructure systems were designed years ago when little or no thought was given to cybersecurity, which makes these systems exceptionally vulnerable. To bring industrial systems up to the level of security necessary to guard against cyberattacks would require enormous financial investments, but experts who are concerned about cyberwarfare say the cost of not doing it is far higher. Langner explains: "It will be definitely more costly if we wait until organized crime, terrorists, or nation states make their move first."[17]

What Is the Best Protection Against Cyberwarfare?

According to many security experts, a crucial first step toward preventing disastrous cyberattacks is to take the threat seriously—which is seldom the case. Says Langner: "After Stuxnet was identified as a weapon, we recommended to every asset owner in America—owners of power plants, chemical plants, refineries and others—to make it a top priority to protect their systems. . . . That wakeup call lasted only about a week." According to Langner, since malware cannot possibly be stopped from spreading through the Internet, computer systems must be protected with tighter security. He explains: "The best option we have to start to counter this threat is to start protecting our systems—control systems especially—in important facilities like power, water, and chemical facilities that produce poisonous gases. Funny thing is, all these control systems, if compromised, could lead to mass casualties, but we still don't have any significant level of cybersecurity for them."[18]

> **Most countries, including the United States, are aware that the smartest way to address cyberwarfare is to make every possible attempt to prevent it.**

Although Langner is correct that critical infrastructure protection has not been a high priority, that is starting to change. US government agencies such as the FBI, DHS, Department of Defense (DOD), and National Security Agency (NSA), are working together toward the mutual goal of protecting critical infrastructures. Partnerships are also being formed among international allies such as the United States, Australia, New Zealand, Canada, and the United Kingdom. In May 2011 US president Barack Obama's administration introduced its International Strategy for Cyberspace, which lays the foundation for addressing the challenges of cyberwarfare while making every attempt to safeguard privacy and the free flow of information.

How Should Governments Respond to Cyberattacks?

Most countries, including the United States, are aware that the smartest way to address cyberwarfare is to make every possible attempt to prevent it. Still, nations throughout the world have begun to develop strategies for how best to respond to major cyberattacks if they happen. In July 2011 the DOD publicized its Strategy for Operating in Cyberspace, which declares that cyberspace will be considered an operational domain like land, sea, air, and space. The Pentagon also announced that it reserves the option of using military force in response to serious cyberattacks. As one military official comments: "If you shut down our power grid, maybe we will put a missile down one of your smokestacks."[19]

The issue of countries using force in retaliation against cyberattacks is fraught with controversy. One of the biggest objections is that the identities of perpetrators are usually unknown, so determining the target for offensive action would likely be based on guesswork. One example of this is the 2007 cyberattacks on the country of Estonia. The attacks were widely assumed to be carried out by Russia, although this was never conclusively proved. In their paper "State Responsibility for Cyber Attacks: Competing Standards for a Growing Problem," Scott J. Shackelford and Richard B. Andres write: "Given the secretive nature of cyber conflict, States may incite civilian groups within their own borders to commit cyber attacks and then hide behind a (however sheer) veil of plausible deniability, thus escaping accountability."[20]

Threats, Questions, and Challenges

Even though security experts disagree about what cyberwarfare is and what it includes, the fact is that cyberattacks are an unfortunate reality throughout the world. As cyberweapons continue to grow more sophisticated and powerful, computer systems will likely be even more threatened than they are today. Through strategic planning, international partnerships, and a renewed focus on making cybersecurity a top priority, a full-scale cyberwar may be avoided—but no one knows whether that will be possible.

What Is Cyberwarfare?

❝There was a time when war was begun with a shot. Now it can begin with the simple click of a mouse. A silent attack that you may never even know occurred until it all unfolds in front of you. This new world goes by the names of cyber security, cyber warfare or cyber terrorism.❞

—Kevin Rudd, Australia's former minister for foreign affairs.

❝As we prepare for cyberwar, one is reminded of the uncertainty faced by medieval mapmakers. As they reached the edge of the known world on their maps they would carefully inscribe on the edge 'here be dragons.' That's just as true of cyberspace today, in more ways than one.❞

—Paul Rosenzweig, an attorney who served with the US Department of Homeland Security and the author of *Cyberwarfare: How Conflicts in Cyberspace Are Challenging America and Changing the World*.

In a September/October 2010 article in the journal *Foreign Affairs*, US deputy secretary of defense William J. Lynn III confirmed an incident that had been a closely guarded secret for over two years: the DOD had suffered the most significant cyberattack ever on its classified military computer networks. The breach was discovered in October 2008 by analysts with the NSA's Advanced Networks Operations team. They detected a mysterious signal emanating from deep within the network—one that harbors top-secret information. This was a likely sign that foreign adversaries had penetrated the classified network with the intention of committing cyberespionage. Military officials viewed it as a grave enough threat for then-president George W. Bush to be informed about it.

Military Cybersecurity Woes

In an investigation called Operation Buckshot Yankee, an elite team of security experts was assembled to analyze the cyberattack. Their biggest puzzle was how the malware had found its way into the classified network, which is considered secure because it is not connected to insecure networks or the Internet. The team found that the infestation had begun with an ordinary portable storage device known as a thumb drive. After being infected by malware, the thumb drive was plugged into an American military laptop by someone stationed at a base in the Middle East. Immediately the infection began to spread, and as it was programmed to do, transferred classified data to servers under foreign control. Says Lynn: "It was a network administrator's worst fear: a rogue program operating silently, poised to deliver operational plans into the hands of an unknown adversary."[21]

In his *Foreign Affairs* article, Lynn refers to the 2008 incident as a "wake-up call" for the Pentagon, one that "marked a turning point in U.S. cyberdefense strategy." It was a much-needed wake-up call because US military networks had been the target of cyberattacks for at least a decade. According to Lynn, the frequency and sophistication of attacks have continued to increase, as he writes: "Adversaries have acquired thousands of files from U.S. networks and from the networks of U.S. allies and industry partners, including weapons blueprints, operational plans, and surveillance data."[22]

> " The Pentagon has significantly tightened security procedures to protect its classified computer systems— yet even this has not stopped cyberattacks. "

Since Lynn's article was published, the Pentagon has significantly tightened security procedures to protect its classified computer systems—yet even this has not stopped cyberattacks. In July 2011 Lynn announced that the network of one of the US military's contractors had been hit with a massive cyberattack the previous March, during which twenty-four thousand confidential documents were stolen. Then in May 2011 the network of a firm that provides intelligence, surveillance, and reconnaissance technology to the US government was attacked, which led to the theft of valuable computer code. Says Lynn: "The cyber threats we face are urgent, sometimes uncertain and potentially devastating as adversaries constantly search for vulnerabilities. . . . In the 21st century, bits and bytes can be as threatening as bullets and bombs."[23]

Operation Shady RAT

Security experts have long known that cyberespionage is a serious and growing problem for computer systems worldwide—and a 2011 report by McAfee shows how glaring the problem is. The investigation, dubbed Operation Shady RAT, was led by Dmitri Alperovitch, the firm's then–vice president of threat research. His team found five years' worth of cyberattacks on seventy-one corporations, government agencies, and non-profit organizations worldwide. The targets included government sites in the United States, Canada, Vietnam, Taiwan, and India, as well as energy and electronics industries, US defense firms, the United Nations Secretariat, and the Olympic committees of three countries. Says Alperovitch: "After painstaking analysis of the logs, even we were surprised by the enormous diversity of the victim organizations and were taken aback by the audacity of the perpetrators."[24]

> According to some security experts, the conflict between Russia and Georgia illustrates how vulnerable wired countries are to assaults that are intended to cripple their networks and cut off communication with the outside world.

According to the McAfee report, the cyberattackers were seeking classified information on US military systems, satellite communications, and data from electronics and natural gas companies, among numerous others. Alperovitch says that the severity of these cyberattacks, combined with how diverse and widespread the victims were, should eliminate any doubt that computer systems throughout the world are vulnerable to cyberattackers. He writes:

> What we have witnessed over the past five to six years has been nothing short of a historically unprecedented transfer of wealth—closely guarded national secrets (including those from classified government networks), source code, bug databases, email archives, negotiation plans and exploration details for new oil and gas field auctions, . . . design schematics, and much more has "fallen off the truck" of numerous, mostly Western companies and disappeared in the ever-growing electronic archives of dogged adversaries.[25]

A Mini-Cyberwar?

Security experts have a wide range of opinions about cyberwarfare, including how threatening it is and whether it exists at all. Those who emphasize that it is an issue of concern often refer to an incident that occurred in the tiny republic of Georgia, which is located south of Russia on the Black Sea. For many years Georgia and Russia have had an adversarial relationship, and in July 2008 tensions escalated into armed conflict—one that also involved cyberattacks.

Several weeks before any shots were fired, a group of hackers assumed to be from Russia launched an assault on Georgia's websites. They seized control of Internet routers that supported online traffic, thus cutting off Georgians' connection to outside news or information sources. Then communication, finance, and government sites were hit with an array of botnets as well as massive DDoS attacks. Richard A. Clarke and Robert K. Knake write: "At their peak, the DDOS attacks were coming from six different botnets using both computers commandeered from unsuspecting Internet users and from volunteers who downloaded hacker software from several anti-Georgia websites. After installing the software, a volunteer could join the cyber war by clicking on a button labeled 'Start Flood.'"[26]

The cyber conflict in Georgia lasted until mid-August 2008. Some experts, such as security expert Rob Rosenberger, dismiss it as relatively minor and not indicative of cyberwarfare. On his exposé site *Vmyths* he writes: "Did a story in the *Wall Street Journal* say 'Thousands of Georgians feared dead in Russian military cyber attack'? NO. Did *The Register* announce 'Russian army hackers make Georgian fuel pipelines flow backward'? NO. . . . Remember this the next time the computer media gets infatuated with the notion of a cyber-war."[27] Those who do not share Rosenberger's perspective argue that the Russian-Georgian conflict was significant because it represents the first case of a cyberspace attack that was synchronized with a major conventional attack.

> Although Conficker has infected an unprecedented number of computers worldwide, its botnet has not caused the kind of catastrophic damage that security experts predicted it would.

Also, according to some security experts, the conflict between Russia and Georgia illustrates how vulnerable wired countries are to assaults that are intended to cripple their networks and cut off communication with the outside world. Says Ronald J. Deibert, who is director of the University of Toronto's research facility Citizen Lab: "In terms of the scope and international dimension of this attack, it's a landmark." Deibert adds that the conflict opens up questions about what constitutes cyberwarfare: "International laws are very poorly developed, so it really crosses a line into murky territory. . . . Is an information blockade an act of war?"[28]

The Mother of All Botnets

When security experts talk about the most troublesome malware ever created, the word *Conficker* is inevitably part of the conversation. Conficker is a computer worm that was first detected in November 2008 at Stanford University. Within a few months of its discovery it had amassed a virtual army of computers to form one of the most menacing botnets in the world—composed of millions of zombie computers. According to Jeffrey Carr, such a massive botnet has untold potential for power and destruction. "One botnet of one million hosts could conservatively generate enough traffic to take most Fortune 500 companies collectively offline," says Carr. "A botnet of 10 million hosts (like Conficker) could paralyze the network infrastructure of a major Western nation."[29] Some security experts take it one step further: Even though it is not likely, they warn that a large and powerful enough botnet could crash the entire Internet.

Although Conficker has infected an unprecedented number of computers worldwide, its botnet has not caused the kind of catastrophic damage that security experts predicted it would. That is a relief but does not alleviate their fear of what is yet to come. No one knows who created the vicious worm, nor does anyone know what its botnet might do in the future. In a March 2009 report by the research institute SRI International, the authors write: "Perhaps the most obvious frightening aspect of Conficker is its clear potential to do harm. Among the long history of malware epidemics, very few can claim sustained worldwide infiltration of multiple millions of infected drones."[30]

As of April 2012 Conficker was still infecting computers worldwide. Microsoft announced in a security report that it had detected a 225 percent increase in infections since 2009 and that Conficker remained the top network threat of all malware. It is somewhat contained, however, because the Conficker Working Group has managed to prevent worm-infected systems from communicating with the worm's creators. The solution seems to be working—at least for now. When or if that will change in the future is not known; thus, no one can possibly predict what the Conficker botnet might do. The authors of the SRI International report write: "Perhaps in the best case, Conficker may be used as a sustained and profitable platform for massive Internet fraud and theft. In the worst case, Conficker could be turned into a powerful offensive weapon for performing concerted information warfare attacks that could disrupt not just countries, but the Internet itself."[31]

Testing the Waters

Any successful cyberattack on a major infrastructure industry could be disastrous, although no one can say for sure whether it will actually happen. Many experts warn, however, that adversaries would be likely to perform a test on a smaller scale first—and according to a few security professionals, that may be what happened at an Illinois water station in November 2011. In a notice posted online, a state terrorism intelligence center reported a cyber intrusion at a plant in Springfield, Illinois. The report stated that a security breach had allowed intruders to manipulate supervisory control and data acquisition system (SCADA) networks that allowed plant operators to perform operations remotely over the Internet. The intrusions had taken place over a period of two to three months, causing a series of minor glitches that gradually escalated and led to the destruction of a water pump at the facility. Based on the internet provider (IP) addresses, the alleged hackers were determined to be from Russia.

> Any successful cyberattack on a major infrastructure industry could be disastrous, although no one can say for sure whether it will actually happen.

As soon as industrial control security expert Joseph Weiss read the report, he posted about it on a blog, and within days the incident became headline news. An article in the *Washington Post* referred to "the first known [cyberattack] to have damaged one of the systems that supply Americans with water, electricity and other essentials of modern life."[32] The DHS, however, downplayed the incident, saying that the claims were based on unconfirmed data that had been leaked to the media. DHS officials were insistent that there was no evidence to support the key details that had been reported, including that the problem at the facility was the result of cyberattack.

Weiss and several other security experts were confused by the DHS's dismissal of the water facility incident, and they wondered if its severity was being intentionally minimized. Says Jim Ivers, an executive with the Rockville, Maryland, industrial security firm Triumfant:

> I find it interesting that DHS and others are warning all of us that industrial control attacks are on the horizon and then go into denial mode when one actually happens within days of the warning. This all begins to feel like field testing for bigger and far more destructive attacks. . . . And no one should be surprised they are doing this field testing on the fringes where systems are bound to be less protected. They can hone their skills to get to the bigger prizes later.[33]

Cyber Uncertainty

From persistent attacks on classified military networks to cyberespionage, the creation of massive botnets, and the complete disabling of computer systems, cyberwarfare has captured the attention of security experts worldwide. They do not always agree on what constitutes cyberwarfare, and some reject the very idea of it. But as battles in cyberspace continue, and cyberweapons grow even more sophisticated and powerful than they are today, only time will tell whether a full-scale cyberwar will become reality.

What Is Cyberwarfare?

66 **Time for a reality check: Cyberwar is still more hype than hazard.**99

—Thomas Rid, "Think Again: Cyberwar," *Foreign Policy*, March/April 2012. www.foreignpolicy.com.

Rid is a lecturer with the Department of War Studies at King's College London, United Kingdom.

66 **Cyberwar is here, and it is here to stay, despite what Thomas Rid and other skeptics think.**99

—John Arquilla, "Cyberwar Is Already Upon Us," *Foreign Policy*, March/April 2012. www.foreignpolicy.com.

Arquilla, who coined the term *cyberwar* in 1993, is an international relations expert and chair of the US Naval Postgraduate School defense analysis department.

66 **The number and sophistication of cyber attacks has increased dramatically over the past five years and is expected to continue to grow.**99

—Gordon M. Snow, "Statement Before the Senate Judiciary Committee, Subcommittee on Crime and Terrorism," Federal Bureau of Investigation, April 12, 2011. www.fbi.gov.

Snow is assistant director of the FBI's Cyber Division.

Bracketed quotes indicate conflicting positions.

* Editor's Note: While the definition of a primary source can be narrowly or broadly defined, for the purposes of Compact Research, a primary source consists of: 1) results of original research presented by an organization or researcher; 2) eyewitness accounts of events, personal experience, or work experience; 3) first-person editorials offering pundits' opinions; 4) government officials presenting political plans and/or policies; 5) representatives of organizations presenting testimony or policy.

❝There have been no cyber wars and perhaps two or three cyber attacks since the Internet first appeared.❞

—James Andrew Lewis, "Cyber Attacks, Real or Imagined, and Cyber War," Center for Strategic and International Studies, July 11, 2011. http://csis.org.

Lewis is director of the Center for Strategic and International Studies Technology and Public Policy program.

❝For the moment, the 'bad guys' have the upper hand— whether they are attacking systems for industrial or political espionage reasons, or simply to steal money— because the lack of international agreements allows them to operate swiftly and mostly with impunity.❞

—Security Defence Agenda, *Cyber-Security: The Vexed Question of Global Rules*, February 2012.

The Security & Defence Agenda is a security and defense think tank headquartered in Brussels, Belgium.

❝Even in an age of intercontinental missiles and aircraft, cyber war moves faster and crosses borders more easily than any form of hostilities in history.❞

—Richard A. Clarke and Robert K. Knake, *Cyber War: The Next Threat to National Security and What to Do About It*. New York: HarperCollins, 2010, p. 201.

Clarke and Knake are cybersecurity and counterterrorism experts who have both served as White House presidential advisers.

❝Cyberspace as a warfighting domain is a very challenging concept.❞

—Jeffrey Carr, *Inside Cyber Warfare: Mapping the Cyber Underworld*. Sebastopol, CA: O'Reilly Media, 2010, p. xiii.

Carr is a cyberintelligence expert who specializes in the investigation of cyberattacks against governments and infrastructures.

❝The traditional idea of warfare and nations conducting warfare using tanks, airplanes, aircraft carriers, etc. does not apply in cyberspace.❞

—Robert M. Lee, "Stuxnet and the Paradigm Shift in Cyber Warfare," Control Global, May 19, 2011. www.controlglobal.com.

Lee is an officer with the US Air Force and an expert on cyberweapons.

❝The cost of entry into this arms race is incredibly low. Furthermore the benefits of attacking someone far outweigh the dangers. This has led to what many are calling a Cyber War.❞

—Jason Andress and Steve Winterfield, *Cyber Warfare: Techniques, Tactics and Tools for Security Practitioners*. Waltham, MA: Syngress, 2011, p. 2.

Andress and Winterfield are cybersecurity experts.

❝For the better part of two decades, analysts have recognized, and feared, the new national vulnerabilities that the information revolution created for the United States.❞

—Eric Sterner, "Retaliatory Deterrence in Cyberspace," *Strategic Studies Quarterly*, Spring 2011. www.au.af.mil.

Sterner is a national security and aerospace consultant based in Washington, DC.

❝Cyberterrorism does not need to deploy forces by ship, plane, or truck. There are no logistical delays or the usual indicators and warnings. Cyber attacks could be used to disable defenses and blind intelligence capabilities in preparation for a devastating kinetic strike.❞

—Tom O'Connor, "The Cyberterrorism Threat Spectrum," DrTomOconnor.com, November 3, 2011. www.drtomoconnor.com.

O'Connor is associate professor of criminal justice/homeland security and the director of the Institute for Global Security at Austin Peay State University in Clarksville, Tennessee.

Facts and Illustrations

What Is Cyberwarfare?

- In an August 2011 survey of over **thirty-three hundred** businesses by the security firm Symantec, the majority of respondents ranked cybersecurity as their top risk, over traditional crime, natural disasters, and terrorism.

- A 2011 report by the National Computer Network Emergency Response Technical Team/Coordination Center of China stated that **35,000** Chinese websites, including 4,635 government sites, were hit by hackers in 2010.

- According to an October 2011 report by the US Government Accountability Office, the number of reported security breaches on US government computers increased **650 percent** between 2006 and 2011.

- In an April 2011 survey by the security technology company McAfee and the Center for Strategic and International Studies, **85 percent** of industry executives said they had experienced network attacks during 2010.

- In a survey published in February 2012 by the Security & Defense Agenda, **57 percent** of cybersecurity specialists said that a global arms race is taking place in cyberspace.

- According to the Department of Defense, the most significant cybersecurity breach in US military history occurred in October 2008 with malware that was dubbed **Agent.btz**.

Companies Lose Millions in Cyberattacks

When asked about cyberattacks on their company networks, information technology professionals surveyed in 2011 said the cost was extraordinary. Nearly half said their companies lost between $250,000 and $1 million in the twelve months before the survey and 15 percent lost up to $2.5 million.

Question: Approximately how much did cyberattacks cost your company over the past 12 months?

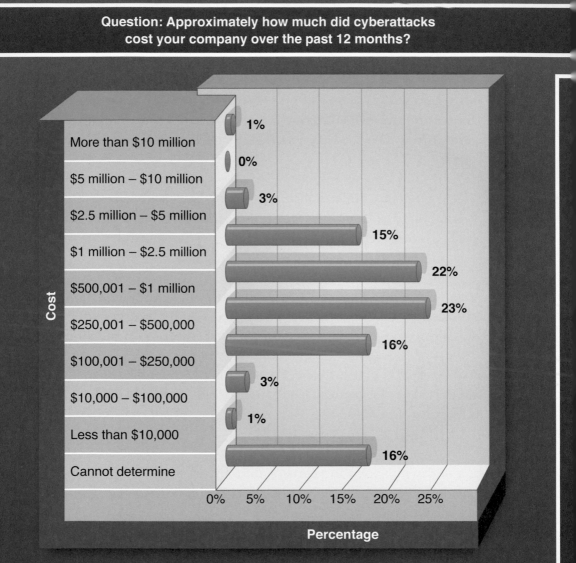

Note: Losses include cash outlays, internal labor, overhead, business disruption, revenue losses, and other expenses related to cyberattacks. Scale goes to 25 percent.

Source: Ponemon Institute, "Perceptions About Network Security," June 2011. www.juniper.net.

Most Cyberattacks Target Government and Public Sector

Phishing is a common method of cyberattack. Phishing involves official-looking e-mails that are laced with malware and sent to specific targets. When attachments are opened, the malware infects the recipient's computer system. This diagram shows the top ten industries affected by phishing-related cyberattacks in 2011.

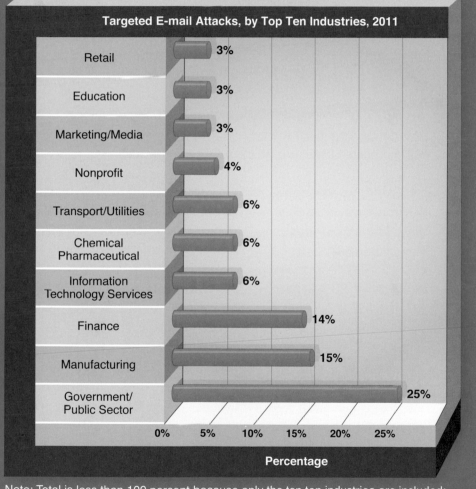

Targeted E-mail Attacks, by Top Ten Industries, 2011

Industry	Percentage
Retail	3%
Education	3%
Marketing/Media	3%
Nonprofit	4%
Transport/Utilities	6%
Chemical Pharmaceutical	6%
Information Technology Services	6%
Finance	14%
Manufacturing	15%
Government/Public Sector	25%

Percentage

Note: Total is less than 100 percent because only the top ten industries are included; scale goes to 25 percent.

Source: Symantec, *Internet Security Threat Report: 2011 Trends*, April 2012. www.symantec.com.

- In a June 2011 survey of information technology professionals by the research firm Ponemon Institute, **22 percent** of respondents said cyberattacks cost their companies from $500,000 to $1 million in the past 12 months.

- According to the authors of a January 2011 report entitled *Reducing Systemic Cybersecurity Risk*, most cyberattacks are caused by **botnets**, which are networks of computers that have been taken over and are remotely controlled by unauthorized parties without the owners' knowledge.

- In an August 2011 survey of over **thirty-three hundred** businesses by the security firm Symantec, **71 percent** of respondents said they experienced a cyberattack in the past year.

- According to a September 2011 report by NPR, as many as **12 million** computers have been infected with malware known as the **Conficker worm**, which turns computer systems into botnets.

- According to Scott Borg, chief economist at the US Cyber Consequences Unit, cyberespionage costs from **$6 billion to $20 billion** annually in the loss of intellectual property and investment opportunities across all industries.

- An October 2011 report by the US Government Accountability Office states that the most prevalent type of security incidents reported by federal agencies was malware such as **viruses or worms**.

- In a June 2011 survey of information technology professionals by the research firm Ponemon Institute, of respondents whose companies had experienced security breaches in the past twelve months, **40 percent** did not know the source of the attacks.

- In an April 2011 report by the security technology company McAfee and the Center for Strategic and International Studies, **25 percent** of industry executives said that in the past twelve months their companies had been victimized by cyberextortion through attack or threat of attack, which was an increase over **20 percent** reported the prior year.

How Great
a Threat Is
Cyberwarfare?

"Criminals are menacing our cyber shores, preparing to launch a large-scale attack. What is clear is that it will happen. What is not obvious is by whom or when."

—William L. Tafoya, a retired FBI special agent who is now a professor in the Information Protection and Security program at the University of New Haven in Connecticut.

"The cyberwar rhetoric is dangerous. Its practitioners are artists of exaggeration, who seem to think spinning tall tales is the only way to make bureaucracies move in the right direction."

—Kevin Poulsen, a notorious "black hat" hacker who gave up the criminal life and is now a *Wired* journalist and consultant on technology and security issues.

After twenty-four years with the FBI, most recently as executive assistant director and "top cybercop," Shawn Henry understands the concept of cyberwarfare better than most. Under his leadership the FBI busted at least eighty notorious hackers affiliated with underground groups such as Anonymous, AntiSec, and LulzSec. Despite these and other victories, however, Henry is convinced that the US government is losing the cyber battle. "We are not winning," he says. "Even though we've had success, the offense outpaces the defense and the problem is getting bigger."[34]

In an April 24, 2012, testimony on cyberthreats before a House of

Representatives subcommittee, Henry was candid about the growing threat of cyberwarfare: "It is difficult to overstate the potential harm these threats pose to our economy, our national security, and the critical infrastructure upon which our country relies." Speaking metaphorically, Henry told the group that just as the bulk of an iceberg's mass is hidden below the water, the same is true of the most sophisticated and damaging cyberthreats. "I would offer that only a very small group of individuals . . . primarily those in the intelligence community," said Henry, "have ever seen 'below the water line,' and the real threat is grossly underappreciated by the public."[35] Henry made it clear that he has, in fact, seen the vast amount of threats that are hidden "below the water line" and that these threats are real, they are imminent, and they need to be taken seriously.

Alarming Vulnerabilities

Also in his testimony, Henry warned about threats to the US critical infrastructure due to advanced technology and the corresponding growth and sophistication of malicious software tools. "New technologies raise new security issues that are not always addressed prior to adoption," he said. "The increasing automation of our infrastructures provides more cyber access points for adversaries to exploit, and the target set grows daily as more and more data is pushed, transmitted, or stored on the network."[36] Henry was referring to an issue that is a top concern for security experts: Growing numbers of industries are running their operations by hooking up their SCADA systems to the Internet.

> Security experts are not the only people who warn about the vulnerability of infrastructure industry systems; hackers are outspoken about it as well.

Research by McAfee and other cybersecurity firms has shown that SCADA systems are prolific in all critical infrastructure industries. This is true for utilities such as electricity, oil, and gas; water treatment and waste management; and the maritime, air, railroad, and automobile traffic control industries. SCADA systems, which have been in operation since the 1960s, are designed to operate from remote locations with little or no human intervention. They automatically collect data from sensors in devices used for industrial processing and store information in databases for central-site management and processing.

The earliest SCADA systems were stand-alone machines that were rarely networked, but that has changed over the years. Today virtually all are connected to the Internet, which markedly increases their vulnerability and risk for cyberattack. Security expert Steve Santorelli explains: "The problem is that all the infrastructure companies are connecting their systems to the Internet, because it never goes down and it's free. They save billions of dollars by switching over from proprietary and older systems. It's not until something goes wrong and kills 100 people that you see the other side of that."[37]

> As innovative and energy-saving as smart grid technology is, it has a downside: vastly increased opportunities for exploitation by cyberattackers.

In the 2011 McAfee/CSIS survey, critical infrastructure industry executives talked about the vulnerability of their SCADA systems. When asked about the Stuxnet worm, which was specifically created to damage and/or destroy industrial control systems, 20 percent of the participants had found it on their systems, with an even higher infection rate in the electrical industry. This was alarming, as the report authors write: "Stuxnet is, in short, a weapon. It is a concrete demonstration that governments will develop malware to sabotage their adversaries' IT systems and critical infrastructure. It also shows that hostile governments can easily target the SCADA systems on which a nation's power, gas, oil, water and sewage systems depend, defeating the defenses upon which most companies rely."[38]

An Unconventional Warning

Security experts are not the only people who warn about the vulnerability of infrastructure industry systems; hackers are outspoken about it as well. One, who uses the screen name pr0f, has often Tweeted about SCADA systems being exceptionally easy for cyberattackers to exploit, and he is convinced that the US infrastructure is in grave trouble because of it. So, when pr0f learned how the DHS had downplayed the November 2011 incident at the Illinois water plant, he found this disturbing. "I was furious at the lack of proper government response," he said in an interview with security company Sophos senior security adviser Chester Wisniewski. "The response they gave was nothing more than 'Nothing happened. Probably.' When clearly something did happen."[39] Pr0f was so frustrated by the dismissal of what he views as a matter of national security that he decided to prove the DHS wrong—by hacking into a SCADA system to show how easily it could be done.

> " Even though cyberattackers are often able to operate anonymously, government officials are fairly certain which countries are behind attacks on the United States. At the top of the list of suspects are China and Russia. "

On November 18, 2011, pr0f broke into what he calls "a really insecure system" at a water plant in South Houston, Texas. After completing his hack, he posted about it on the Pastebin website and included links to screenshots showing diagrams of the facility. He made it clear that he would not expose any details that could be used by cyberattackers, nor had he caused any harm to the machinery at the plant. "I don't really like mindless vandalism," he wrote. "It's stupid and silly." Yet despite pr0f's aversion to causing harm, he had a blunt accusation for infrastructure industries: "On the other hand, so is connecting interfaces to your SCADA machinery to the Internet."[40]

How Smart Are "Smart" Technologies?

In the 2011 McAfee/CSIS survey, participants were asked questions about new technologies, and smart grid was mentioned often. Smart grid technology is designed to help control energy use. It uses a two-way stream of information that allows an electrical supplier to monitor and control the flow of electricity to homes and businesses, which helps conserve electricity during peak times when it is most in demand. The Environmental Defense Fund, which is enthusiastic about smart grid technology, explains:

Traditionally, electricity has been delivered via a one-way street: Energy from a big, central station power plant is transmitted along high-voltage lines to a substation, and from there to your house. A smart grid turns those lines into a two-way highway. Wireless smart meters measure and communicate—in real time—information about how much energy you're using and what it costs, allowing you to better manage your consumption, carbon footprint and bill.[41]

As innovative and energy-saving as smart grid technology is, it has a downside: vastly increased opportunities for exploitation by cyberattackers. Critical infrastructure systems are already vulnerable because of lax security measures, and industry experts warn that smart grid technology makes this situation much worse. It expands network control to households and even individual appliances, which creates more access points from which to launch attacks. Henry says that new smart grid technologies must be developed and implemented in ways that also provide protection from unauthorized use. "Otherwise," he writes, "each new device could become a doorway into our systems for adversaries to use for their own purposes."[42] Security experts say that with smart grid technology, a cyberattacker could conceivably hack into a system from a remote location and cut off power at whim.

Despite the potential risks involved, many people view smart grid technology as the answer to the world's energy shortage and the wave of the future. Thus, it is experiencing a great deal of growth, as the McAfee/CSIS report states: "Plans to exercise far more precise control over consumers' use of electricity has aroused great

> In an October 2011 report to Congress called *Foreign Spies Stealing US Economic Secrets in Cyberspace,* the Office of the National Counterintelligence Executive reveals details about cyberthreats that were formerly classified information.

enthusiasm among government policymakers, particularly in China and the United States."[43] The report goes on to explain that 56 percent of the executives whose companies were planning new smart grid systems also planned to connect to the Internet. Although most of these companies were aware that the systems would increase vulnerabilities to their networks, only two-thirds said they had adopted special security measures for the smart grid controls. This, say security experts, is the sort of carelessness that puts the US infrastructure at risk.

Presumed Adversaries

Even though cyberattackers are often able to operate anonymously, government officials are fairly certain which countries are behind attacks on the United States. At the top of the list of suspects are China and Russia, largely because they are known to have the knowledge, resources, capability, and motivation to create sophisticated cyberweaponry. Says Dennis Blair, the former director of national intelligence: "Over the past several years, we have seen cyberattacks against critical infrastructures abroad, and many of our own infrastructures are as vulnerable as their foreign counterparts. A number of nations, including Russia and China, can disrupt elements of the U.S. information infrastructure."[44]

In an October 2011 report to Congress called *Foreign Spies Stealing US Economic Secrets in Cyberspace*, the Office of the National Counterintelligence Executive reveals details about cyberthreats that were formerly classified information. The authors of the report state that Chinese cyberattackers "are the world's most active and persistent perpetrators of economic espionage. United States private sector firms and cybersecurity specialists have reported an onslaught of computer network intrusions that have originated in China, but [intelligence experts] cannot confirm who was responsible." The report also touts Russia's cyberintelligence capabilities, saying that the country is aggressively pursuing activities to collect economic information and technology from targets in the United States. The authors also make a chilling prediction for the future: "We judge that the governments of China and Russia will remain aggressive and capable collectors of sensitive US economic information and technologies, particularly in cyberspace."[45]

Renowned security technologist Bruce Schneier, who is often referred to as a security guru, does not dispute that other countries are exploiting US computer systems, nor does he deny that China poses an intelligence threat to the United States. His complaint is that government officials and many security experts are referring to these cybercrimes as acts of war, which he says grossly exaggerates the actual threat. He explains: "The threats are real; the threats are serious; cyber space is not a safe place, but these are not war threats. For the threat of cyber war to be serious means you believe that the threat of war is serious. And if you're not worried about war . . . you can't be worried about cyber war; that just doesn't make any sense."[46]

A Call for Cool Heads

Amidst the loud chorus of security experts, government officials, and others who warn about the looming threat of cyberwar, people who share Schneier's views are somewhat outnumbered. Yet they are convinced that even though cyberattacks are indeed a serious problem, that is very different from saying the world is a mouse click away from cyberwar. Jerry Brito and Tate Watkins, who are with George Mason University's Mercatus Center, discuss this in an April 2011 paper. They write: "The notion that our power grid, air traffic control system, and financial networks are rigged to blow at the press of a button would be terrifying if it were true. But fear should not be a basis for public policy making."[47]

Brito and Watkins refer to government reports warning that the United States is losing the battle in cyberspace, which they claim are not backed up with solid evidence. Citing the Department of Defense's reports of military networks being probed on hundreds of thousands of occasions, they write: "Probing and scanning networks are the digital equivalent of trying doorknobs to see if they are unlocked—a maneuver available to even the most unsophisticated would-be hackers." In the conclusion of their paper, Brito and Watkins acknowledge the importance of cybersecurity, but offer words of caution: "The alarmist rhetoric coming out of Washington that focuses on worst-case scenarios is unhelpful and dangerous."[48]

The Great Unknown

Cyberattacks are becoming an unfortunate fact of life. With insufficient security measures in place and more industries connecting to the Internet, critical infrastructure operations are a frequent target—even hackers warn about their vulnerability. Whether the increasing threats are significant enough to be considered cyberwarfare is a matter of contention, with some experts saying the attacks themselves are proof enough, and others arguing that this is alarmist rhetoric. Although no one knows for sure who is right and who is wrong, the truth is likely somewhere in the middle.

How Great a Threat Is Cyberwarfare?

> 66 **Someone has started a cyber war and we all have to take it seriously. If we don't, our jobs, our companies, our critical systems and perhaps our lives could become collateral damage.** 99

—Eric J. Byres, "I Was Wrong," Tofino Security blog, September 17, 2010. www.tofinosecurity.com.

Byres is a computer security expert and founder of Byres Security in British Columbia, Canada.

> 66 **It is unlikely that there will ever be a true cyberwar.** 99

—Peter Sommer and Ian Brown, *Reducing Systemic Cybersecurity Risk*, Organisation for Economic Co-operation and Development, January 14, 2011. www.oecd.org.

Sommer is with the London School of Economics, and Brown is a senior research fellow at the Oxford Internet Institute.

Bracketed quotes indicate conflicting positions.

* Editor's Note: While the definition of a primary source can be narrowly or broadly defined, for the purposes of Compact Research, a primary source consists of: 1) results of original research presented by an organization or researcher; 2) eyewitness accounts of events, personal experience, or work experience; 3) first-person editorials offering pundits' opinions; 4) government officials presenting political plans and/or policies; 5) representatives of organizations presenting testimony or policy.

> **We have to continue to focus on the threat of cyber-attacks. We're now in a very different world, where we could face a cyber-attack that could be the equivalent of Pearl Harbor.**

—Leon Panetta, "Remarks by Secretary Panetta to Service Members at US Strategic Command," US Department of Defense, August 5, 2011. www.defense.gov.

Panetta is the US secretary of defense.

> **There was no and there is no Pearl Harbor of cyber war.**

—Thomas Rid, "Cyber War Will Not Take Place," *Journal of Strategic Studies*, February 2012. www.tandfonline.com.

Rid is a lecturer with the Department of War Studies at King's College London, United Kingdom.

> **The consequences of cyberwar are too dire for the United States to wait and learn from our mistakes. If we begin losing the cyberbattles frequently, it may mean the end of America as we know it.**

—Erika Andersen, "Morning Bell: Time for America to Get Cyber-Serious," *Foundry* (blog), Heritage Foundation, June 6, 2011. http://blog.heritage.org.

Andersen is a senior digital communications associate at the Heritage Foundation.

> **Stop the apocalyptic rhetoric. The alarmist scenarios dominating policy discourse may be good for the cybersecurity-industrial complex, but they aren't doing real security any favors.**

—Jerry Brito and Tate Watkins, "Wired Opinion: Cyberwar Is the New Yellowcake," *Wired*, February 14, 2012. www.wired.com.

Brito is director of the Technology Policy Program at George Mason University's Mercatus Center, and Watkins is a research associate with the same group.

66 Not only will we see more state-sponsored attacks in cyberspace, but we also will also see more non-state attacks from groups possessing powerful technology and software. 99

—Robert M. Lee, "Stuxnet and the Paradigm Shift in Cyber Warfare," Control Global, May 19, 2011. www.controlglobal.com.

Lee is an officer with the US Air Force and an expert on cyberweapons.

66 Malicious actors ranging from criminals and miscreants to terrorists and nation-states have exploited cyberspace vulnerability for a wide range of purposes. Attacks on commercial systems are a daily occurrence, and it is rare for more than a few days to pass before some company announces it has been attacked. 99

—Eric Sterner, "Retaliatory Deterrence in Cyberspace," *Strategic Studies Quarterly*, Spring 2011. www.au.af.mil.

Sterner is a national security and aerospace consultant based in Washington, DC.

66 It is difficult to overstate the potential impact these threats pose to our economy, our national security, and the critical infrastructure upon which our country relies. 99

—Gordon M. Snow, "Statement Before the Senate Judiciary Committee, Subcommittee on Crime and Terrorism," Federal Bureau of Investigation, April 12, 2011. www.fbi.gov.

Snow is assistant director of the FBI's Cyber Division.

66 It's not hyperbole which prompted the US to equate hacker attacks with an invasion—they clearly understand the possible consequences. The more we look at it, the scarier it gets. 99

—Eugene Kaspersky, "Call for Action: Internet Should Become a Military-Free Zone," *Nota Bene* (blog), November 25, 2011. http://eugene.kaspersky.com.

Kaspersky is an Internet security expert from Russia.

How Great a Threat Is Cyberwarfare?

- In a survey published in February 2012 by the Security & Defence Agenda, **84 percent** of cybersecurity specialists said that cyberattacks threaten national and international security as well as trade.

- In an August 2011 survey of over **thirty-three hundred** businesses by the security firm Symantec, the majority of respondents ranked cybersecurity as their top threat, over traditional crime, natural disasters, and terrorism.

- In a June 2011 survey of information technology professionals by the research firm Ponemon Institute, **46 percent** of respondents said a successful exploit of their organization's network was likely over the next twelve months, and **23 percent** said it was very likely.

- According to Gordon M. Snow, assistant director of the FBI's Cyber Division, the most significant cyberthreats to the United States are those most likely to cause **injury or death** to US citizens, to illicitly acquire **assets**, or to illegally obtain **sensitive or classified** US military intelligence or **economic information**.

- In an April 2011 report by the security technology company McAfee and the Center for Strategic and International Studies, over **40 percent** of industry executives said they expected a major cyberattack within a year.

China Viewed as Biggest Cyberattack Threat

Security experts say that critical infrastructure industries are vulnerable to cyberattack. A 2011 survey of power, oil, gas, and water industry executives from fourteen countries found that over half of their companies had been attacked by other governments. As this graph shows, the country viewed as most threatening is China.

Question: What country is of greatest concern in the context of network attacks on your country or sector?

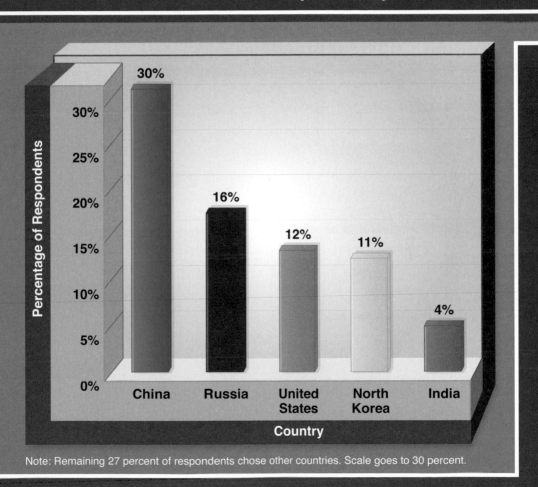

Note: Remaining 27 percent of respondents chose other countries. Scale goes to 30 percent.

Source: Stewart Baker, Natalia Filipiak, and Katrina Timlin, *In the Dark*, McAfee/Center for Strategic and International Studies, 2011. www.mcafee.com.

Cyberwarfare Viewed as Real Threat

During a debate in June 2010, an audience at a Washington, DC, venue heard from leading cybersecurity experts, two of whom claimed that the threat of cyberwar is exaggerated and two of whom denounced that viewpoint. Audience members were polled before and after the presentations and by the end of the evening, nearly three-fourths were convinced that the threat is real.

The Cyberwar Threat Has Been Grossly Exaggerated

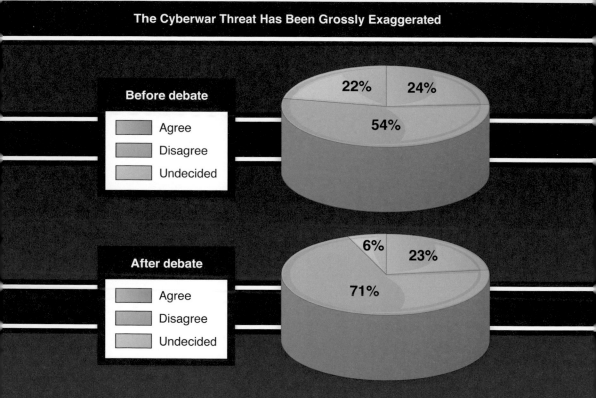

Before debate

- Agree
- Disagree
- Undecided

22% 24% 54%

After debate

- Agree
- Disagree
- Undecided

6% 23% 71%

Source: Intelligence Squared, "The Cyber War Threat Has Been Grossly Exaggerated," June 8, 2010. http://intelligencesquaredus.org.

- According to January 2012 testimony by National Intelligence Director James R. Clapper, **China and Russia** are considered major cyberthreats to the United States, as entities within the countries have been responsible for extensive illegal intrusions into US computer networks and theft of US intellectual property.

Utility Industries Threatened by Cyberattack

To gauge the level of threat facing critical infrastructure industries, a research firm conducted a survey of information technology professionals from utility and energy companies. Only 5 percent of respondents thought there was no chance of their companies being the target of a successful cyberattack in the next year.

Question: What is the likelihood of a successful exploit on your organization's network in the next twelve months?

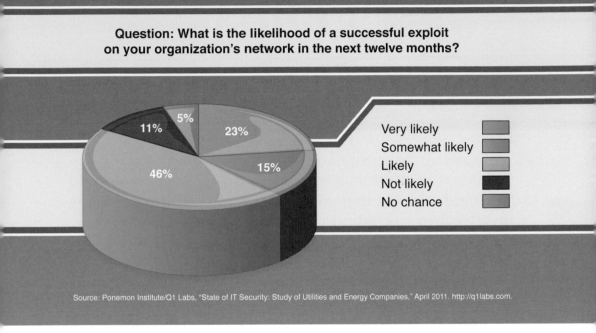

Source: Ponemon Institute/Q1 Labs, "State of IT Security: Study of Utilities and Energy Companies," April 2011. http://q1labs.com.

- In a June 2011 survey of information technology professionals by the research firm Ponemon Institute, **77 percent** of respondents said that cyberattacks against their company became more severe or more difficult to detect or contain in the previous twelve to eighteen months.

- According to a 2011 report for the Congressional Research Service, the **Stuxnet worm** is the first malware specifically designed to target the networked industrial control systems of utilities, and could have implications for the severity of future cyberattacks.

What Is the Best Protection Against Cyberwarfare?

> **"We need to continue to develop partnerships within industry, academia, and across all of government to have a dramatic improvement in our ability to share intelligence to combat this threat."**
>
> —Shawn Henry, retired executive assistant director of the FBI, now president of the security firm CrowdStrike.

> **"There is a risk that as the government partners more closely with private industry, sensitive personal information may be improperly or inadvertently disclosed."**
>
> —The Constitution Project, which seeks to reform America's criminal justice system and strengthen the rule of law through policy reforms, advocacy, and public education.

In late September 2011, in the control room of Acme Specialty Chemical Corporation, a systems operator noticed that something was wrong with his computer. It had slowed down and was acting sluggish, which was a warning sign of a network problem. Seconds later the room went dark—all lights were out and every monitor screen was black. As security staff ran from computer to computer in a futile effort to bring the system back up, pumps suddenly started running on their own as though controlled by an outside force. "There's nothing we can do," an operator told the company's horrified CEO. "We can only sit here and watch it happen."[49]

The chemical company does not exist and the computer system meltdown never really happened. The "crisis" was a mock disaster staged by the DHS at its national laboratory in Idaho Falls, Idaho. The purpose of the drill was to show how a massive cyberattack could crash the network of a critical infrastructure company—and if it did, how control operations would be rendered useless and attackers would assume command. Even though the incident was staged, members of the media who witnessed it were stunned to learn how a powerful cyberweapon like Stuxnet could be used to destroy an industrial facility. A November 2011 NPR report explains: "If this mock facility were an actual chemical plant, hazardous liquids could be spilling. If it were an electric utility, the turbines could be spinning out of control. If it were a refinery, the tanks could be bursting or pipelines could be blowing up, all because the cyberattackers have been able to take over the computer network that controls the key operations."[50]

Cybersecurity from the Ground Up

Because infrastructure industries are known to be vulnerable to cyberattack, experts worldwide stress that tight security measures are absolutely critical. One of the problems revealed by executives during the 2011 McAfee/CSIS survey was that system security was an afterthought rather than a priority early in the networks' development. One participant was blunt in saying that computer systems were not designed with security in mind; security measures were tacked on later rather than built in at the start. This is now considered an unsophisticated, risky approach, and avoiding it was the thinking behind a testing facility known as DETERlab.

A joint venture between the University of Southern California and the University of California at Berkeley, DETERlab is a five-hundred-computer scientific laboratory where researchers, security companies, and students can

> " Because infrastructure industries are known to be vulnerable to cyberattack, experts worldwide stress that tight security measures are absolutely critical. "

> **The majority of infrastructure industries in the United States are privately owned and operated, so many security experts believe that preventing cyberwarfare requires a coordinated effort between government and private enterprise.**

conduct experiments with hardware and software to test for security flaws. It is a sealed off "mini-Internet" where experimenters, tapping into the network from remote locations, can run cyberattack simulations without posing any risk to the actual Internet. Says Terry Benzel, a DETERlab supervisor who is with the University of Southern California's Information Science Institute: "If what we're trying to do is test something which breaks the Internet or breaks network security in an enterprise, we give you an environment to be able to do that in a safe way."[51]

One experiment researchers conducted at DETERlab was a scale representation of the Slammer worm, which began to spread in 2004 and was the fastest-moving worm in history. As it raced through the Internet, Slammer doubled in size every 8.5 seconds, infecting over 90 percent of vulnerable host computers within ten minutes. The DETERlab experiment allowed researchers to study the same kinds of effects in a controlled environment, which can help them design network security that resists such an attack before it strikes.

Synergy Through Partnering

The majority of infrastructure industries in the United States are privately owned and operated, so many security experts believe that preventing cyberwarfare requires a coordinated effort between government and private enterprise. Gordon M. Snow, who is assistant director of the FBI's Cyber Division, says that such partnerships can make a significant difference in thwarting cyberattacks. "The FBI has developed strong relationships with private industry and the public," says Snow. "InfraGard is a premier example of the success of public-private partnerships. Under this initiative, state, local, and tribal law enforcement, academia, other government agencies, communities, and private industry work with us through our field offices to ward off attacks against critical infrastructure."[52] Snow's mention of InfraGard refers to a partnership that focuses on information sharing between the public and private sector with the goal of protecting infrastructure industries from cyberattack.

The benefit of partnerships between private industry and government agencies was discussed during the 2011 McAfee/CSIS survey. Executives from Japan, China, and the United Arab Emirates reported having high levels of interaction between government and private owners of infrastructure industries. In contrast, participants from the United States and United Kingdom said their infrastructure industries had little or no partnership arrangements with government agencies. The report authors opine: "Government can encourage security by collaborating with industry—and by adopting regulations that demand better security than the market does."[53]

In May 2011 the NSA and three major Internet service providers (ISPs) announced that they had embarked on a trial partnership. The unique program is based on the philosophy that the whole is greater than the sum of its parts: ISPs have the ability to filter massive amounts of Internet traffic, while the NSA has a wealth of knowledge about malicious code and cyberattacks. The partners believe that combining these areas of strength will provide a greater level of protection and better cyberspace security. Jim Dempsey, who is vice president for public policy at the Center for Democracy and Technology, calls the arrangement an "elegant solution to the long-standing problem of how to apply the government's special expertise while avoiding domestic surveillance by the government."[54]

A Proverbial Hornet's Nest

Because of his enthusiasm about the collaborative effort and his hope that such voluntary arrangements could be the wave of the future, Dempsey was especially disturbed to learn that the government was pursuing a different solution: legislation that would allow network operators to freely share information with the government. This, according to Dempsey, has the potential to be a gross violation of privacy laws. He writes:

> Instead of helping private network operators become better at the job they are already doing, the Administration

has sent legislation to Congress that would create a blanket exception to all privacy laws, allowing the network operators to share information about any and all communications with the government and placing responsibility in the government to do the analysis. The Administration proposal could result in a flood of private traffic flowing to the government.[55]

Dempsey is referring to the Cyberintelligence Sharing and Protection Act (CISPA), which was introduced to Congress in November 2011. If signed into law, CISPA would allow ISPs to share information with government agencies such as the DHS and NSA about threats that are detected on the Internet. Also under the law, ISPs may share data with each other if they believe it will accelerate their ability to extinguish a cyberattack.

Supporters of the legislation claim that it will facilitate much-needed information sharing, while allowing companies threatened by online attacks to report network intrusions to the government; in turn, they will get prompt assistance without having to deal with unnecessary bureaucratic red tape. US representative Dutch Ruppersberger, who cosponsored the bill, says that the legislation is a "decisive first step" in tackling the looming threat of cyberwarfare. "Without important, immediate changes to American cybersecurity policy," says Ruppersberger, "I believe our country will continue to be at risk for a catastrophic attack to our nation's vital networks—networks that power our homes, provide our clean water or maintain the other critical services we use every day."[56]

Organizations such as the Center for Democracy and Technology, Electronic Frontier Foundation, and American Civil Liberties Union have condemned the CISPA legislation.

Organizations such as the Center for Democracy and Technology, Electronic Frontier Foundation, and American Civil Liberties Union have condemned the CISPA legislation. Their argument is that the bill allows—and even encourages—ISPs to arbitrarily share Internet users' private information with each other and with the government. Allowing this free sharing of information, opponents claim, flies in the face of US privacy laws. Under CISPA, an ISP would not be required to shield any personal identifying data on its customers; all that is required is for the ISP to believe a threat exists, which opponents say is highly subjective. They also claim that CISPA will open the door for potential abuse, such as federal authorities reading private e-mails, social networking posts, and text messages under the guise of protecting national security.

On April 26, 2012, the US House of Representatives approved the legislation and forwarded it to the Senate for a vote. President Barack Obama has spoken out about his opposition to CISPA on the grounds that it would infringe on the privacy of Internet users, and he threatened a veto if the law made it to his desk.

More Legislation Controversy

Obama and the legislators who oppose CISPA are determined to strengthen US cybersecurity, but they have proposed a different method of achieving it: by giving more decision-making power to the DHS. To remedy the fact that system security for most privately owned critical infrastructure industries is not subject to government regulation, the legislative group introduced the Cybersecurity Act of 2012. Under this law, the DHS would have the authority to determine which private infrastructure companies are most critical to national security and require that they meet specified security standards.

According to US senator Joseph I. Lieberman, who cosponsored the bill, the Cybersecurity Act would strengthen America's cyber defense in many ways. One of the most important would be ensuring the security of computer systems that control the most critical infrastructure industries. "Privately owned and operated cyber infrastructure can well be and probably someday will be the target of an enemy attack," says Lieberman. "Today it is the target of economic exploitation and we've got to work with the private sector to better secure those systems, both for their own defense and for our national defense." Lieberman goes on to say that federal security standards will only apply to companies "that if brought down or commandeered would lead to mass casualties, evacuations of major population centers, the collapse of financial markets, or significant degradation of security. So this is a tight and high standard."[57]

A number of legislators oppose the proposed law, saying that it puts an unnecessary burden on businesses by subjecting them to costly regulations. Many owners of private infrastructure industries agree, such as Robert Johnston, the president and chief executive officer of MEAG Power in Atlanta, Georgia. "There's been an awful lot written about cyber security and the threat of it," says Johnston. "There are a lot of people who want to spend a huge amount of money on something that we have not necessarily identified. There have been some hackings into some certain systems around the country, but show me an event where we've lost systems due to cyber terrorism. I'm not aware of one."[58]

> Whether the answer is better network design, partnerships, more information sharing, or some combination of them all, protection against cyberattacks is a must.

Many security experts view perspectives such as Johnston's as a clear lack of understanding about how serious the threat of cyberwarfare is. They claim that because owners of critical infrastructure industries grossly underestimate their vulnerability to cyberattacks, they are unlikely to take the necessary steps to make their systems more secure. In fact, investigations have shown that operators at many critical infrastructure companies have no idea that their industrial control systems are accessible through the Internet.

This has been an eye-opening experience for Sean McGurk, who is director of the DHS's National Cybersecurity and Communications Integration Center. During personal visits to hundreds of US power stations, water treatment facilities, and other infrastructure industries, McGurk has witnessed that operators were not aware of an Internet connection. He explains: "In every case, we were told that the systems were completely isolated from the enterprise network or the Internet, that there were no direct connections. And in no case has that ever been true. In hundreds of vulnerability assessments, we've always found connections between the equipment on the manufacturing floor and the outside world."[59]

Challenges and Hope

Whether the answer is better network design, partnerships, more information sharing, or some combination of them all, protection against cyberattacks is a must. Although the problem may seem insurmountable, many security experts are hopeful that solutions are within reach and that cyberwarfare can be stopped before it starts. Says Shawn Henry: "I am optimistic that by strengthening partnerships, effectively sharing intelligence, and successfully identifying our adversaries, we can best protect businesses and critical infrastructure from grave damage."[60]

What Is the Best Protection Against Cyberwarfare?

66 **The biggest secret in the world about cyber war may be that at the very same time the U.S. prepares for offensive cyber war, it is continuing policies that make it impossible to defend the nation effectively from cyber attack.** 99

—Richard A. Clarke and Robert K. Knake, *Cyber War: The Next Threat to National Security and What to Do About It.* New York: HarperCollins, 2010, p. xi.

Clarke and Knake are cybersecurity and counterterrorism experts who have both served as White House presidential advisers.

66 **If we are to pursue the type of regulation of Internet service providers and utilities that Clarke and Knake advocate, we should demand more precise evidence of the threat against which we intend to guard, and of the probability that such a threat can be realized.** 99

—Jerry Brito and Tate Watkins, "Loving the Cyber Bomb? The Dangers of Threat Inflation in Cybersecurity Policy," Mercatus Center, April 2011. http://mercatus.org.

Brito is director of the Technology Policy Program at George Mason University's Mercatus Center, and Watkins is a research associate with the same group.

* Editor's Note: While the definition of a primary source can be narrowly or broadly defined, for the purposes of Compact Research, a primary source consists of: 1) results of original research presented by an organization or researcher; 2) eyewitness accounts of events, personal experience, or work experience; 3) first-person editorials offering pundits' opinions; 4) government officials presenting political plans and/or policies; 5) representatives of organizations presenting testimony or policy.

66 When people of a nation do not feel secure, they look to their government to protect them; if the government cannot, then the people look towards change in the government. 99

—Robert M. Lee, "Stuxnet and the Paradigm Shift in Cyber Warfare," Control Global, May 19, 2011. www.controlglobal.com.

Lee is an officer with the US Air Force and an expert on cyberweapons.

66 We need to hold the government accountable to spend our tax dollars wisely in the cyber warfare realm, not to just throw dollars in the air and hope they will land where they will do some good. 99

—Stephen Northcutt, "Foreword," in Jason Andress and Steve Winterfield, *Cyber Warfare: Techniques, Tactics and Tools for Security Practitioners*. Waltham, MA: Syngress, 2011, p. xxi.

Northcutt is president of the SANS Institute, a cybersecurity graduate school located in Bethesda, Maryland.

66 Governments can facilitate partnerships with critical infrastructure operators to share best practice, threat updates and analysis, and data on attacks. 99

—Peter Sommer and Ian Brown, *Reducing Systemic Cybersecurity Risk*, Organisation for Economic Co-operation and Development, January 14, 2011. www.oecd.org.

Sommer is with the London School of Economics, and Brown is a senior research fellow at the Oxford Internet Institute.

66 Our national cybersecurity policy is at a critical juncture; the steady stream of recent high profile cyberattacks serves as a constant reminder that U.S. policymakers have yet to carve out a unified, workable cybersecurity strategy. 99

—Jim Dempsey, "Don't Mess with Success," Center for Democracy & Technology, June 17, 2011. www.cdt.org.

Dempsey is vice president for public policy at the Center for Democracy and Technology.

66 Considering the fact that peace and world stability strongly relies on the Internet, an international organization needs to be created in order to control cyber-weapons. A kind of International Atomic Energy Agency but dedicated to the cyberspace. 99

—Eugene Kaspersky, "Call for Action: Internet Should Become a Military-Free Zone," *Nota Bene* (blog), November 25, 2011. http://eugene.kaspersky.com.

Kaspersky is an Internet security expert from Russia who founded the cybersecurity firm Kaspersky Lab.

....

66 A cyber strategy that persists in segregating cyber attackers into existing legal and policymaking frameworks . . . only ensures that the U.S. will always be a step behind. Individual attacks may occur in milliseconds. 99

—Eric Sterner, "Stuxnet and the Pentagon's Cyber Strategy," George C. Marshall Institute, October 13, 2010. www.marshall.org.

Sterner is a national security and aerospace consultant based in Washington, DC.

....

66 We are optimistic that by strengthening relationships with our domestic and international counterparts, the FBI will continue to succeed in identifying and neutralizing cyber criminals, thereby protecting U.S. businesses and critical infrastructure from grave harm. 99

—Gordon M. Snow, "Statement Before the Senate Judiciary Committee, Subcommittee on Crime and Terrorism," Federal Bureau of Investigation, April 12, 2011. www.fbi.gov.

Snow is assistant director of the FBI's Cyber Division.

....

Facts and Illustrations

What Is the Best Protection Against Cyberwarfare?

- According to an April 2012 report by Symantec, the security firm blocked over 5.5 billion malicious attacks in 2011, an increase of more than **81 percent** over 2010.

- In a June 2011 survey of information technology professionals by the research firm Ponemon Institute, **55 percent** of respondents felt that security planning was not given sufficient emphasis and funding within their organizations.

- An October 2011 report by the US Government Accountability Office found that the primary cause of information security weaknesses was the **non-implementation** of an agency-wide security program.

- According to Kevin Groberg, senior counsel of the House of Representatives Homeland Security Committee, **partnerships need to be strengthened** between the Department of Defense and the defense industry in order to maximize cyberattack prevention.

- In a survey published in February 2012 by the Security & Defence Agenda, **Israel, Sweden, and Finland** were determined to be the most prepared to deal with cyberattacks, while **Mexico** was the least prepared.

- According to the authors of a January 2011 report entitled *Reducing Systemic Cybersecurity Risk*, strategies to reduce the impact of a successful cyberattack should be part of **business planning** for all firms.

Cybercrime Defense Readiness

In 2011 the Security & Defence Agenda conducted a global survey to evaluate cyber-readiness, or the ability of countries to withstand sophisticated cyberattacks by adversaries. The global security experts surveyed rated Finland, Israel, and Sweden as most prepared and Mexico least prepared.

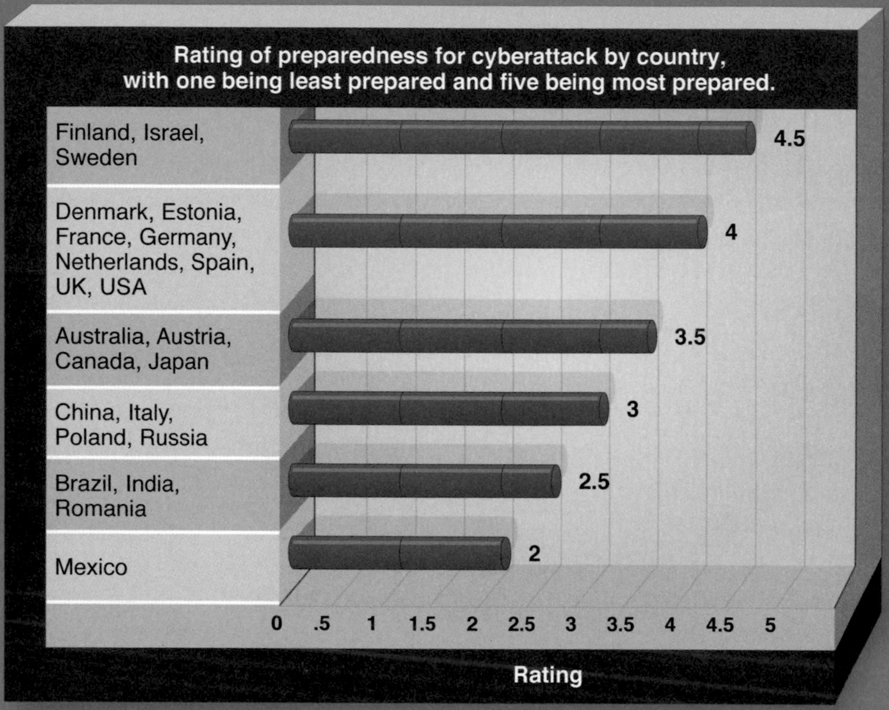
Rating of preparedness for cyberattack by country, with one being least prepared and five being most prepared.
Finland, Israel, Sweden
4.5
Denmark, Estonia, France, Germany, Netherlands, Spain, UK, USA
4
Australia, Austria, Canada, Japan
3.5
China, Italy, Poland, Russia
3
Brazil, India, Romania
2.5
Mexico
2
0 .5 1 1.5 2 2.5 3 3.5 4 4.5 5
Rating

Note: No country was rated lower than 2 or higher than 4.5.

Source: Brigid Grauman, "Cyber-Security: The Vexed Question of Global Rules," Security & Defence Agenda, February 2012. www.securitydefenceagenda.org.

- In an August 2011 survey of over thirty-three hundred businesses by the security firm Symantec, **45 percent** of respondents said their companies were doing well or extremely well at pursuing innovative or cutting-edge security solutions.

- In a survey published in February 2012 by the Security & Defence Agenda, nearly **70 percent** of cybersecurity specialists said the United States and other countries should create regulations designed to deter cyberattacks.

Security Lagging in Critical Infrastructure Industries

In a 2011 survey of infrastructure industry executives, McAfee asked questions about the adoption of new security measures that can help companies defend their networks against cyberattack. The survey found the largest improvement in the water and sewage industries, but little change in other industries surveyed. Overall, the McAfee researchers concluded, adoption of security measures is growing but not keeping pace with the increase in threats and vulnerabilities.

Measuring Improvement: Security Measure Adoption Rates

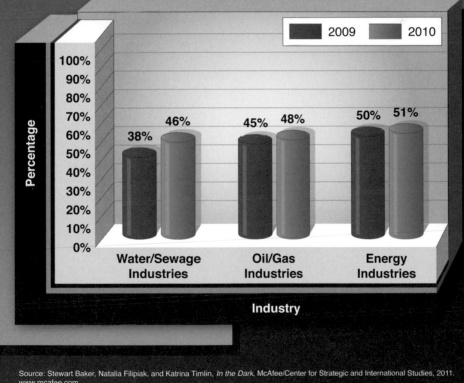

Source: Stewart Baker, Natalia Filipiak, and Katrina Timlin, *In the Dark*, McAfee/Center for Strategic and International Studies, 2011. www.mcafee.com.

- In an August 2011 survey of over thirty-three hundred businesses by the security firm Symantec, **41 percent** of respondents said that cybersecurity is more important today than it was a year ago.

Security Not a High Priority for Many Organizations

Cybersecurity experts stress that cyberattacks can be thwarted when computer systems are amply protected, but many organizations are deficient in that area. This was revealed during a 2011 survey of information technology professionals from a wide range of industries. Fifty-five percent of those surveyed said that security planning was not a high enough priority at their organizations.

Question: Do you feel that security planning is given sufficient emphasis and funding within your organization?

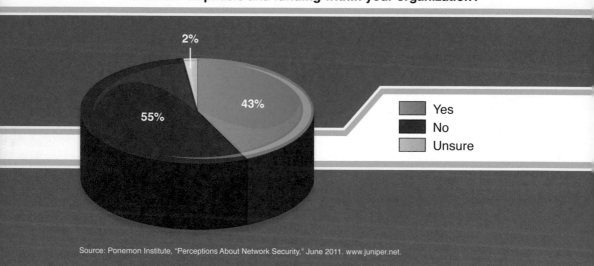

Source: Ponemon Institute, "Perceptions About Network Security," June 2011. www.juniper.net.

- According to the authors of a January 2011 report entitled *Reducing Systemic Cybersecurity Risk*, the most immediately effective action that governments can take is to **improve the security standards** of their own critical information systems.

- In a survey published in February 2012 by the Security & Defence Agenda, only **20 percent** of respondents from the private sector said their organizations were taking part in cybersecurity exercises or taking adequate precautions.

How Should Governments Respond to Cyberattacks?

66Governments are beginning to understand that the Internet can be a highway to hell, and are waking up to the need to do something about it.99

—Eugene Kaspersky, an Internet security expert from Russia who founded the cybersecurity firm Kaspersky Lab.

66Here's hoping that, amid the looming havoc of cyberwars to come, there will also be prospects for cyberpeace.99

—John Arquilla, an international relations expert and chair of the US Naval Postgraduate School Defense Analysis Department.

In March 2011 members of the Obama administration and US military officials engaged in an intense discussion about a grave topic. America was about to join North Atlantic Treaty Organization (NATO) allies in a military strike on Libya in an effort to stop the brutal dictator Moammar Gadhafi from inflicting violence on civilians. A massive air strike was planned, but the group debated using a different approach at first: launching a cyberattack to cripple the Libyan government's computer systems and bring down their air defense network.

Due to a number of complex challenges, the cyberwarfare plan was scrapped. One of the most formidable hurdles was the significant amount of time it would take to crack into Libya's computer network, search for vulnerabilities, and then write and insert malicious code. James Andrew Lewis explains: "It's the cyberequivalent of fumbling around in the dark until you find the doorknob. It takes time to find the vulnerabilities. Where is the thing that I can exploit to disrupt the network?" Another reason the group decided against the cyberattack was the potential fallout from such an action. If the United States launched the attack, this could set a precedent for other countries such as Russia and China—who are known to have cyberweaponry capabilities—to launch attacks of their own, possibly against the United States. Says Lewis: "We don't want to be the ones who break the glass on this new kind of warfare."[61]

A Virtual Battlefield

With cyberwarfare considered one of the most ominous threats, the United States has devoted a great deal of time planning for how best to address it—and the strategy is to play hardball with adversaries. In a May 2011 report entitled the *International Strategy for Cyberspace*, the White House makes it clear that if warranted, the United States will not hesitate to respond to hostile acts in cyberspace with the same force that would be used for any other threat to the country. As William J. Lynn III explains: "It should come as no surprise that the United States is prepared to defend itself in all domains. It would be irresponsible, and a failure of the Defense Department's mission, to leave the nation vulnerable to a known threat. Just as the military defends itself against hostile acts from land, air, and sea, it must also be prepared to respond to hostile acts in cyberspace."[62]

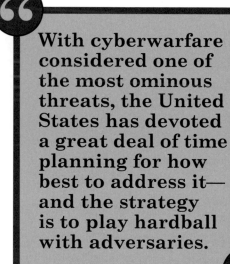

With cyberwarfare considered one of the most ominous threats, the United States has devoted a great deal of time planning for how best to address it— and the strategy is to play hardball with adversaries.

After publication of the White House document, the Pentagon released its own report in which cyberspace is referred to as the fifth operational domain, along with land, sea, air, and space. This clarification reinforces the military's conviction that it has the right—and the responsibility—to defend its computer systems and networks just as it defends American soil. Says Eric Sterner, a national security and aerospace consultant: "Unlike the air, land and sea domains, we lack dominance in cyberspace and could grow increasingly vulnerable if we do not fundamentally change how we view this battle-space."[63]

According to Nick Harvey, the armed forces minister of the United Kingdom, British military officials share America's vision for defending the cyberspace domain. In 2010 Britain released a national security strategy that warned of the inevitability of cyberwarfare and emphasized the importance of the country's military being prepared to fight a cyberspace battle. Harvey says that even though cyberspace is a new domain, "its use in warfare should be subject to the same strategic and tactical thought as existing means. Action in cyberspace will form part of the future battlefield, but it will be integrated rather than separate, complementary rather than alternative. . . . Cyber will be part of a continuum of tools with which to achieve military effect, both defensive and otherwise, and will be an integral part of our armoury." Harvey goes on to stress the importance of international partnerships and cooperation in defending cyberspace: "We need to think and act internationally because cyberspace is international space and the rules that govern it will be international too."[64]

> Even without definitive proof . . . American military strategists and many cybersecurity experts are convinced that China is one of the main perpetrators of cyberattacks on US systems.

Denouncing America's Strategy

Although military officials and many US leaders have expressed their approval of the Pentagon's get-tough approach to cyberwarfare, this is not true of everyone. In a paper published soon after the White House announcement in 2011, Benjamin H. Friedman and Christopher Preble condemned the cyberwarfare plan, saying that a military response to cyberattacks is "preposterous." Friedman, who is a research fellow in defense and homeland security studies, and Preble, the Cato Institute's director of foreign policy studies, explain their perspective: "The policy threatens to repeat the overreaction and needless conflict that plagued American foreign policy in the past decade. It builds on national hysteria about threats to cybersecurity, the latest bogeyman to justify our bloated national security state."[65]

Friedman and Preble go on to say that the term *cyberattack* has never been well defined and is vague, which will inevitably lead to confusion over which cyberspace acts are punishable by military force. Also, they contend, launching a war to retaliate for acts such as cyberespionage, which does not involve violence or death, seems disproportionate. In the majority of cases, whether cyberattackers were serving the government or operating based on their own motives is unclear. "Taken literally," they write, "the new policy might have us risking nuclear exchange with Russia because it failed to stop teenagers in Moscow Internet cafés from attacking Citibank.com."[66]

Hunting Down the Bad Guys

One of the biggest challenges of the retaliation approach to cyberwarfare is the uncertainty of who the perpetrators are. Assigning blame for a cyberattack is often impossible even for the most seasoned cyber sleuths, because those with malicious intent can easily hide their tracks in cyberspace. According to Jeffrey Carr, attribution is a problem for everyone who seeks to avenge an act of cyberwar. "I'm not aware that that problem has been solved yet," says Carr. "Until it is, who are we shaking our sabers at?" Carr adds that the attribution dilemma seriously increases the likelihood for mistaken identity. "How do we know that the country we suspect is behind any given attack hasn't been set up to take the fall?" Carr asks. "It's a relatively simple matter to plant clues within the code or utilize code strings that are known signatures of a particular hacker group with national allegiances."[67]

Many attacks are assumed to be sanctioned by nation-states,

> " In terms of cyberwarfare, adversaries who consider launching a massive cyberattack against a country might be deterred by the threat of the nation's military launching a counter-cyberattack. "

but this is difficult for anyone to know for sure. Even without definitive proof, however, American military strategists and many cybersecurity experts are convinced that China is one of the main perpetrators of cyberattacks on US systems. This presumption is based on the fact that China has demonstrated advanced cyber capabilities in recent years. According to security expert Eugene Kaspersky, China is one of the countries with a dedicated cyber force and is developing cyberweapons. Also, China was considered the primary culprit in the massive number of cyberespionage cases identified during the McAfee study Operation Shady RAT. In a January 2012 opinion piece, Lynn, along with former director of national intelligence Mike McConnell and former secretary of defense Michael Chertoff write: "The Chinese government has a national policy of economic espionage in cyberspace. In fact, the Chinese are the world's most active and persistent practitioners of cyber espionage today. Evidence of China's economically devastating theft of proprietary technologies and other intellectual property from U.S. companies is growing."[68]

> " The use of powerful cyber superweapons such as Stuxnet would be permissible only if the US president grants approval, even if used during a time of hostilities. "

Chinese government officials vehemently deny that they are to blame for any cyberattacks, including cyberespionage. Wang Baodong, a spokesman for the Chinese Embassy in Washington, told the *Wall Street Journal* that the Chinese government opposes "any crime, including hacking, that destroys the Internet or computer network" and has laws in place that ban the practice. In fact, says Baodong, China has been ready and willing to cooperate with other countries to counter such attacks. He claims, however, that the effort has been hindered because "some people overseas with Cold War mentality are indulged in fabricating the sheer lies of the so-called cyberspies in China."[69]

Deterrence Through Fear

A term that is common among members of the military is *deterrence*, which refers to enemies resisting the urge to attack out of fear of retaliation. In terms of cyberwarfare, adversaries who consider launching a massive cyberattack against a country might be deterred by the threat of the nation's military launching a counter-cyberattack. With the United States' new cyberspace strategy, the deterrence effect would be twofold: Adversaries could expect to be on the receiving end of a cyberattack combined with a kinetic attack, meaning one that uses traditional weaponry. Lewis refers to this as "cross-domain" deterrence, saying that "no nation would launch a cyber-only attack against the United States because of the threat of retaliation."[70]

In his 2011 paper "Retaliatory Deterrence in Cyberspace," Sterner points out that deterrence could make significant contributions to America's security in cyberspace. "Deterrence is ingrained in US national security posture," he writes. "It dominated Cold War debates and thinking about preventing Soviet aggression against vital US national interests. The lack of a direct US-Soviet war seemed to confirm its utility. Indeed, with the collapse of Soviet communism, deterrence advocates continued to proclaim its primary value in preventing aggression." Sterner emphasizes, however, that a cyberspace policy of deterrence is unique, and warrants careful thought, because "traditional models of deterrence have little relevance to cyberspace." He goes on to say that the United States must develop a deterrence strategy specifically for cyberspace. The plan would revolve around the US commitment to retaliate against cyberattacks using a combination of cyberweapons and traditional weapons. Says Sterner: "Those cyberspace actors contemplating attacks on the United States will have to consider the potential punishment that such an attack might invite."[71]

Stocking the Cyber Arsenal

As part of its new cyberspace strategy and to better identify how the United States engages in cyberwarfare, the Pentagon has developed a classified list of cyberweapons and cyber tools, such as malware designed to sabotage an adversary's critical computer networks. An essential part of this strategy is a framework that spells out what the weapons are and establishes when they can be used, which is similar to the DOD's guidelines for traditional weapons. Says one military official: "So whether it's a tank, an M-16 or a computer virus, it's going to follow the same rules so that we can understand how to employ it, when you can use it, when you can't, what you can and can't use."[72]

The framework for use of cyberweaponry makes a number of clarifications, not only about when it can and cannot be used but also when presidential authorization is necessary. It mandates that the use of powerful cyber superweapons such as Stuxnet would be permissible only if the US president grants approval, even if used during a time of hostilities. Also, the use of any cyberweapon must be proportional to the threat and not inflict excessive collateral damage or cause civilian casualties. A specific mandate is that the military must obtain authorization from the US president before it can penetrate a foreign computer network and insert malware to be activated later. Military officials do not need such approval to penetrate foreign networks for other activities such as analyzing the cyberwarfare capabilities of a suspected adversary or analyzing how computer networks operate. Also without presidential authorization, military cyber soldiers may leave beacons to mark spots in a network that can later be targeted for insertion of malware.

Tough Choices

It is safe to say that no one, even top military leaders, want full-scale cyberwarfare to happen. As with traditional kinds of war, damage, destruction, and loss of lives could result from it. Still, cyberspace has proved to be a realm that invites malicious, threatening behavior and the use of cyberweapons that are created for the sole purpose of causing harm. As a result, planning for how to respond to cyberattacks is a necessary part of a country's strategy for defense. Exactly what those response mechanisms should be is a matter of controversy, and will likely remain so for many years to come.

How Should Governments Respond to Cyberattacks?

" The United States reserves the right, under the law of armed conflict, to respond to serious cyberattacks with an appropriate, proportional, and justified military response. "

—William J. Lynn III, "The Pentagon's Cyberstrategy, One Year Later," *Foreign Affairs*, September 28, 2011. www.foreignaffairs.com.

Lynn is the US deputy secretary of defense.

" The idea of responding militarily to most of these threats is preposterous. . . . We do not threaten to bomb countries caught spying on us in traditional ways and should not do so just because the prefix 'cyber' applies. "

—Benjamin H. Friedman and Christopher Preble, "A Military Response to Cyberattacks Is Preposterous," Cato Institute, June 2, 2011. www.cato.org.

Friedman is a research fellow in defense and homeland security studies, and Preble is director of foreign policy studies at Cato Institute.

Bracketed quotes indicate conflicting positions.

* Editor's Note: While the definition of a primary source can be narrowly or broadly defined, for the purposes of Compact Research, a primary source consists of: 1) results of original research presented by an organization or researcher; 2) eyewitness accounts of events, personal experience, or work experience; 3) first-person editorials offering pundits' opinions; 4) government officials presenting political plans and/or policies; 5) representatives of organizations presenting testimony or policy.

❝ If you are going to throw cyber rocks, you had better be sure that the house you live in has less glass than the other guy's, or that yours has bulletproof windows. ❞

—Richard A. Clarke and Robert K. Knake, *Cyber War: The Next Threat to National Security and What to Do About It*. New York: HarperCollins, 2010, p. 209.

Clarke and Knake are cybersecurity and counterterrorism experts who have both served as White House presidential advisers.

❝ Daily crackers and terrorists are skulking, battering firewalls, and learning more each time they do so. Clearly, preparations to thwart such attacks are necessary. ❞

—William L. Tafoya, "Cyber Terror," *FBI Law Enforcement Bulletin*, November 2011. www.fbi.gov.

Tafoya is a retired FBI special agent who is now a professor in the Information Protection and Security program at the University of New Haven in Connecticut.

❝ One of the most heavily debated issues in international law is when states may lawfully respond to cyber attacks in self-defense. ❞

—Matthew J. Sklerov, "Introduction," in Jeffrey Carr, *Inside Cyber Warfare: Mapping the Cyber Underworld*. Sebastopol, CA: O'Reilly Media, 2010, p. 45.

Sklerov is a lieutenant commander with the US Navy.

❝ Information security and cyberwarfare planners in the Pentagon have noted both in doctrine and in informal channels that a good offensive cyber operations capability is the best defense. ❞

—Catherine A. Theohary and John Rollins, *Terrorist Use of the Internet: Information Operations in Cyberspace*, Congressional Research Service, March 8, 2011. www.fas.org.

Theohary is an analyst in national security policy and information operations, and Rollins is a specialist in terrorism and national security.

66 In terms of cyber attacks the one overwhelming characteristic is that most of the time it will be impossible for victims to ascertain the identity of the attacker— the problem of attribution. This means that a defence doctrine based on deterrence will not work. 99

—Peter Sommer and Ian Brown, *Reducing Systemic Cybersecurity Risk*, Organisation for Economic Co-operation and Development, January 14, 2011. www.oecd.org.

Sommer is with the London School of Economics, and Brown is a senior research fellow at the Oxford Internet Institute.

66 Governments cannot contain these cyber threats singlehandedly through domestic measures alone. Neither should governments be left to grapple with this danger on their own any longer, as the expertise and skill to combat these cyber threats are largely dispersed across the globe. 99

—International Multilateral Partnership Against Cyber-Threats (IMPACT), "Mission & Vision," 2012. www.impact-alliance.org.

Based in Malaysia, IMPACT brings together governments, academia, and industry experts to enhance the world's capabilities in dealing with cyber threats.

How Should Governments Respond to Cyberattacks?

- In 2011 the Pentagon announced that as part of its first formal cyberstrategy, certain types of cyberattacks on the United States would be considered an act of war deserving of **military retaliation**.

- A survey published in February 2012 by the Security & Defence Agenda found that only four countries (the United States, Israel, China, and Russia) and the United Kingdom have proven **offensive cyberattack capabilities**.

- In 2011 the North Atlantic Treaty Organization (NATO) implemented a Policy on Cyber Defence, which encompasses planning and capability development, as well as **coordinated assistance** if one of its allies is victimized by a cyberattack.

- According to cybersecurity and counterterrorism expert Richard A. Clarke, **defending the United States** from cyberattacks should be the first goal of a cyberwar strategy.

- According to Eric Sterner, a cybersecurity expert with the George C. Marshall Institute, the greatest challenge involved with retaliating against a cyberattack is **identifying the attacker and appropriate targets**.

US Response to Cyberattacks

In May 2011 the White House issued an *International Strategy for Cyberspace*, which declared that the United States would defend against cyberattacks by another country using whatever means were deemed justified—including military force.

US deterrence strategy: To ensure that the risks associated with attacking America's networks vastly outweigh the potential benefits.
Criminals and other non-state actors who threaten national and economic security by intruding on or disrupting networks at home or abroad will be investigated, apprehended, and prosecuted.
Consistent with applicable international law, the United States will respond to hostile acts in cyberspace in the same way as other threats, including diplomatic, informational, and economic means.
After exhausting all possible options, and weighing the costs and risks of action against the costs and risks of inaction, the United States reserves the right to use military force in retaliation for cyberattacks.

Source: White House, *International Strategy for Cyberspace*, May 2011. www.whitehouse.gov.

- To protect and defend the US military's computer and communications systems, the Department of Defense created an agency called the **Cyber Command**, which began full operations in 2010.

- According to the authors of a January 2011 report entitled *Reducing Systemic Cybersecurity Risk*, one of the biggest problems with using military force against cyberwarfare is that many likely targets will be **civilians**.

- In a survey published in February 2012 by the Security & Defence Agenda, the majority of respondents felt that cybersecurity should be considered part of a country's **military defense**.

Support for Forceful Military Response

After the White House announcement that the United States would use military force against countries that launch serious cyberattacks, the research group Rasmussen Reports conducted a poll of 1,000 American adults. Half of the respondents agreed that a major cyberattack should be viewed as a act of war deserving of military retaliation.

Question: Should a major cyberattack on the United States by another country be viewed as an act of war, justifying a forceful military response?

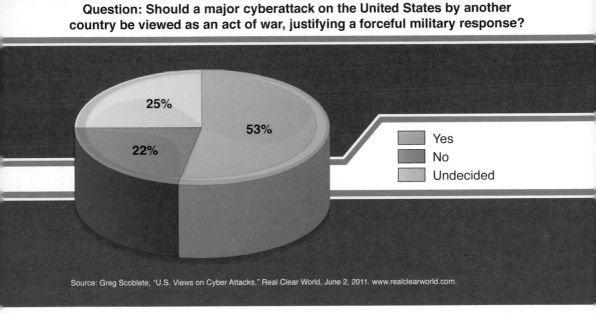

Source: Greg Scoblete, "U.S. Views on Cyber Attacks," Real Clear World, June 2, 2011. www.realclearworld.com.

- In an April 2011 report by the security technology company McAfee and the Center for Strategic and International Studies, **over half** of respondents said they were confident that their government authorities were capable of addressing cyberattacks.

- In an April 2011 report by the security technology company McAfee and the Center for Strategic and International Studies, over **80 percent** of respondents from Brazil and **70 percent** from Mexico felt their governments were not capable of addressing cyberattacks.

Public Supports Offensive Tactics, Sanctions in Response to Cyberespionage

After news reports about McAfee's 2011 investigation of 72 global countries victimized by cyberespionage, Reuters conducted an online poll. When asked how countries should respond to such cyberattacks, more than half of the respondents supported retaliating either with force or through economic sanctions.

Question: What should be the priority in the wake of the biggest series of cyberattacks?

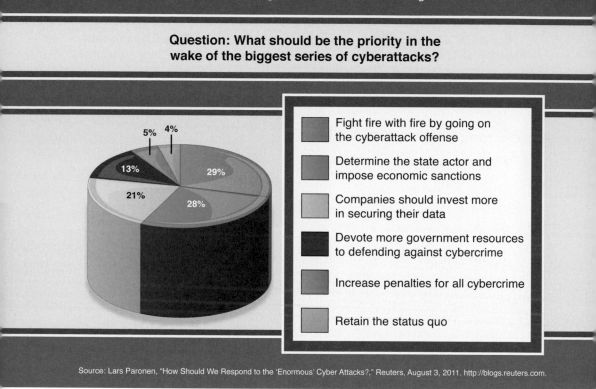

Fight fire with fire by going on the cyberattack offense

Determine the state actor and impose economic sanctions

Companies should invest more in securing their data

Devote more government resources to defending against cybercrime

Increase penalties for all cybercrime

Retain the status quo

Source: Lars Paronen, "How Should We Respond to the 'Enormous' Cyber Attacks?," Reuters, August 3, 2011. http://blogs.reuters.com.

- According to cybersecurity and counterterrorism expert Richard A. Clarke, **North Korea** and **Russia** have the greatest ability to withstand cyberwar, whereas the United States has the lowest.

- In a survey published in February 2012 by the Security & Defence Agenda, **over one-third** of respondents said that cybersecurity is more important than missile defense.

Key People and Advocacy Groups

Tim Berners-Lee: A computer expert from England who created the software, browser, and server that became the World Wide Web.

Jerry Brito: Director of the Technology Policy Program at George Mason University and known for his viewpoint that the cyberwarfare threat is overly exaggerated.

Jeffrey Carr: A cyberintelligence expert who specializes in the investigation of cyberattacks against governments and infrastructures and is the author of *Inside Cyber Warfare: Mapping the Cyber Underworld.*

Richard A. Clarke: A cybersecurity expert who served three US presidents as counterterrorism adviser and then founded the cybersecurity firm Good Harbor Consulting.

Department of Homeland Security: An agency of the US government whose mission is to protect the country from all threats, including threats related to cyberwarfare.

Electronic Frontier Foundation: A civil liberties organization dedicated to defending free speech, privacy, and consumer rights on the Internet and is opposed to cybersecurity legislation that interferes with these rights.

Shawn Henry: A retired FBI executive assistant director and "top cybercop" who is now president of the cybersecurity firm CrowdStrike.

Eugene Kaspersky: An Internet security expert from Russia who founded the internationally renowned cybersecurity firm Kaspersky Lab.

Ralph Langner: An industrial systems security expert from Germany who was the first to analyze the Stuxnet worm's programming code and discover that it was designed to attack and destroy a specific target.

William J. Lynn III: The US secretary of defense and a staunch proponent of policies that encourage information sharing and aggressively attack the problem of cyberwarfare.

National Security Agency: An agency of the US Department of Defense whose mission is to prevent foreign adversaries from gaining access to sensitive or classified national security information, including through cyberattack.

Kevin Poulsen: A notorious "black hat" hacker who gave up the criminal life and is now a journalist and consultant on technology and security issues, and who is skeptical about cyberwarfare being a viable threat.

Thomas Rid: A lecturer at the Department of War Studies at King's College London, United Kingdom, and a noted skeptic about the threat of cyberwar.

Marc Rotenberg: The president of the Electronic Privacy Information Center, an organization that denounces any cybersecurity legislation that infringes on Internet users' right to free speech and privacy.

Andrey Sablenikov: A famous Russian cybersecurity expert who is suspected of being the mastermind behind at least one massive botnet.

Bruce Schneier: An internationally renowned security technologist who has often been called a cybersecurity guru and who believes that the threat of cyberwar has been overblown and is alarmist rhetoric.

Joseph Weiss: An industry expert on control systems and the type of cybersecurity that best protects them.

Chronology

1969
A successful first test of ARPANET (Advanced Research Projects Agency Network) proves that computers can be linked together to communicate with each other; this experiment marks the birth of the Internet.

1982
The first known computer virus, Elk Cloner, is developed and unleashed by a ninth grader named Rich Skrenta, who intended it as a practical joke.

1990
British computer expert Tim Berners-Lee announces the development of software, a point-and-click browser, and the world's first Web server, marking the official launch of the World Wide Web.

1993
International relations experts John Arquilla and David Ronfeldt coin the term *cyberwar* to describe the emerging form of knowledge-based conflict.

1970   **1980**

1990

1983
Members of a hacking group called the 414s are arrested for breaking into sixty US government computer systems, including the New Mexico nuclear research facility Los Alamos National Laboratory.

1988
A worm released to demonstrate flaws in Internet protocol spreads out of control, crashing computers throughout the United States.

1989
In the first cyberespionage case to make international headlines, a group of West German hackers are arrested for breaking into the US government computer network and selling operating system source code to the Soviet state security agency.

1994
In a *Wired* magazine article, Brown University professor James Der Derian coins the term *cyber deterrence* in reference to the fight against information warfare.

1999
The North Atlantic Treaty Organization (NATO) unintentionally bombs the Chinese embassy in Belgrade, Yugoslavia, which incites a wave of cyberattacks from China against US government websites.

2000

The most serious reported attack against a critical infrastructure to date occurs in Australia when a hacker breaks into a waste management computer system and alters pump station operations, causing thousands of gallons of raw sewage to spill into local parks, rivers, and creeks.

2008

An attack on the Pentagon's classified computer systems is called the most significant cybersecurity breach in US military history.

2010

Cybersecurity experts confirm that the computer worm Stuxnet is the world's first known cyber super-weapon because it was designed specifically to seek and destroy real-world machinery.

2003

The White House publishes its *National Strategy to Secure Cyberspace*; the US Department of Homeland Security forms the National Cyber Security Division to protect US government computer systems from Internet-based attacks.

2000

2010

2007

Hackers assumed to be linked to the Russian government unleash a wave of cyber-attacks that crash the websites of Estonia's government agencies, media, and banks.

2011

The US Department of Defense unveils its new *Strategy for Operating in Cyberspace*, which includes reserving the option of using military force in response to serious cyberattacks.

2001

After a Chinese fighter jet collides with a US military spy aircraft over the South China Sea, thousands of Chinese hackers launch a cyberattack against the United States for what they perceive to be an act of aggression.

2009

Officials from the Pentagon announce the creation of a Cyber Command, which will be responsible for protecting US military computer networks from cyberattacks.

2012

After cyberattacks against Iran's oil industry, Iranian officials blame the United States, Israel, and the United Kingdom for trying to ruin their country's economy.

Related Organizations

Center for Democracy and Technology (CDT)

1634 I St. NW, Suite 1100
Washington, DC 20006
phone: (202) 637-9800 • fax: (202) 637-0968
e-mail: info@cdt.org • website: www.cdt.org

The CDT is dedicated to preserving the openness of the Internet, ensuring freedom of expression online, and protecting privacy. Its website features an Internet Openness Standards section as well as information about cybersecurity, cyberterrorism, and legislation that the group considers a potential infringement of constitutional rights.

Council on Foreign Relations

Harold Pratt House
58 E. Sixty-Eighth St.
New York, NY 10065
phone: (212) 434-9400 • fax: (212) 434-9800
e-mail: communications@cfr.org • website: www.cfr.org

The Council on Foreign Relations is an independent, nonpartisan organization that offers a variety of publications, interviews, and interactives, as well as a search engine that produces numerous articles about cyberwarfare.

Electronic Frontier Foundation (EFF)

454 Shotwell St.
San Francisco, CA 94110
phone: (415) 436-9333 • fax: (415) 436-9993
e-mail: info@eff.org • website: www.eff.org

The EFF is a civil liberties organization dedicated to defending free speech, privacy, and consumer rights on the Internet, and is opposed to cybersecurity legislation that interferes with any of these rights. Its website offers white papers, legal cases, archived news releases, and a link to the *DeepLinks* blog, as well as a number of articles about cybersecurity.

Related Organizations

George C. Marshall Institute

1601 North Kent St., Suite 802
Arlington, VA 22209
phone: (571) 970-3180 • fax (571) 970-3192
e-mail: info@marshall.org • website: www.marshall.org

The George C. Marshall Institute is devoted to advancing public policy that is based on scientific facts. The "Cybersecurity" section of its website offers numerous publications about cyberwarfare, as well as video and news articles.

Intelligence and National Security Alliance (INSA)

Ballston Metro Center Office Towers
901 North Stuart St., Suite 205
Arlington, VA 22203
phone: (703) 224-4672 • fax: (703) 224-4681
website: http://insaonline.org

The INSA is an intelligence and national security organization that offers news releases, fact sheets about cyberwarfare, the *INSA Insider* newsletter, and a search engine that produces numerous publications about cybersecurity and related issues.

International Multilateral Partnership Against Cyber Threats (IMPACT)

Jalan IMPACT
63000 Cyberjaya
Malaysia
phone: +60 (3) 8313 2020 • fax: +60 (3) 8319 2020
e-mail: contactus@impact-alliance.org
website: www.impact-alliance.org

IMPACT brings together industry experts, governments, and academia to enhance the world's capabilities in dealing with cyberthreats. Its website offers the *IMPACT Insider* online newsletter, news articles, and a resource center with a variety of publications related to cybersecurity.

North Atlantic Treaty Organization (NATO)

Boulevard Leopold III
1110 Brussels
Belgium
phone: +32 2 707 84 85 • fax: +32 2 707 87 70
website: www.nato.int

NATO's fundamental purpose is to safeguard the freedom and security of its members. Numerous publications and reports about cyberwarfare and cyberterrorism are available on the "Newsroom" section of its website.

Organisation for Economic Co-operation and Development (OECD)

2 rue André Pascal
75775 Paris Cedex 16
France
phone: +33 1 45 24 82 00 • fax: +33 1 45 24 85 00
website: www.oecd.org

The OECD's mission is to promote policies that will improve the economic and social well-being of people throughout the world. Its website's search engine produces a number of articles and reports about cyberwarfare, cybersecurity, cyberterrorism, and related issues.

Security & Defence Agenda (SDA)

Parc Léopold
137 rue Belliard
1040 Brussels
Belgium
phone: +32 2 737 91 48 • fax: +32 2 736 32 16
e-mail: info@securitydefenceagenda.org
website: www.securitydefenceagenda.org

The SDA is a specialist security and defense think tank. The "Cyber Initiative" section of its website features video presentations, a cyberattack logbook, a cyber reference library, and a link to the comprehensive February 2012 report *Cyber-Security: The Vexed Question of Global Rules*.

US Department of Defense (DOD)

1400 Defense Pentagon
Washington, DC 20301
phone: (703) 571-3343
website: www.defense.gov

The DOD website search engine produces a wealth of information about cybersecurity, cyberwarfare, and cyberterrorism.

US Department of Homeland Security (DHS)

245 Murray Dr. SW, Building 410
Washington, DC 20528
phone: (202) 282-8000
website: www.dhs.gov

The "Cybersecurity" section of the DHS website offers reports and publications, and the site's search engine produces numerous articles about cyberwarfare and cyberterrorism.

US Government Accountability Office (GAO)

441 G St. NW
Washington, DC 20548
phone: (202) 512-3000
e-mail: contact@gao.gov • website: www.gao.gov

The GAO is an independent, nonpartisan watchdog agency that reports to Congress and investigates how the federal government spends taxpayer dollars. Numerous publications and reports about cybersecurity and cyberwarfare are available through its website's search engine.

US National Security Agency (NSA)

9800 Savage Rd., Suite 6248
Ft. George G. Meade, MD 20755
phone: (301) 688-6524 • fax: (301) 688-6198
e-mail: nsapao@nsa.gov • website: www.nsa.gov

The NSA's mission is to prevent foreign adversaries from gaining access to sensitive or classified national security information, including through cyberattack. Its website offers news releases, articles, speeches and testimonies, and a search engine that produces numerous articles related to cybersecurity and cyberwarfare.

For Further Research

Books
Jason Andress and Steve Winterfield, *Cyber Warfare: Techniques, Tactics and Tools for Security Practitioners*. Waltham, MA: Syngress, 2011.

Mark Bowden, *Worm: The First Digital World War*. New York: Atlantic Monthly, 2011.

Joel Brenner, *America the Vulnerable: Inside the New Threat Matrix of Digital Espionage, Crime, and Warfare*. New York: Penguin, 2011.

Jeffrey Carr, *Inside Cyber Warfare: Mapping the Cyber Underworld*. Sebastopol, CA: O'Reilly Media, 2010.

Ananda Mitra, *Digital Security: Cyber Terror and Cyber Security*. New York: Chelsea House, 2010.

Richard Stiennon, *Surviving Cyberwar*. Lanham, MD: Government Institutes, 2010.

Periodicals
Devlin Barrett, "U.S. Outgunned in Hacker War," *Wall Street Journal*, March 28, 2012.

Richard A. Clarke, "Cyber Attacks Can Spark Real Wars," *Wall Street Journal*, February 16, 2012.

Mark Clayton, "From the Man Who Discovered Stuxnet, Dire Warnings One Year Later," *Christian Science Monitor*, September 22, 2011.

John C. Dvorak, "Cybersecurity and False Hope," *PC Magazine*, March 6, 2012.

Michael Joseph Gross, "Enter the Cyber-Dragon," *Vanity Fair*, September 2011.

John Hudson, "The Pentagon Is Confused About How to Fight a Cyberwar," *National Journal*, June 1, 2011.

Stew Magnuson, "Pentagon Criticized for Not Doing More to Protect Homeland from Cyberattacks," *National Defense*, December 2010.

Mike McConnell, Michael Chertoff, and William J. Lynn III, "China's

Cyber Thievery Is National Policy—and Must Be Challenged," *Wall Street Journal*, January 27, 2012.

Eric Pfanner, "Apocalypse in Cyberspace? It's Overdone," *New York Times*, January 16, 2011.

Michael Riley, "The Code War," *Bloomberg Businessweek*, July 25–July 31, 2011.

Michael S. Schmidt, "New Interest in Hacking as Threat to Security," *New York Times*, March 13, 2012.

Hayley Tsukayama, "CISPA: Who's for It, Who's Against It, and How It Could Affect You," *Washington Post*, April 27, 2012.

Kirsten Weir, "Power Struggle: A Cyber Attack Could Disable the Grid That Delivers Electricity to the United States," *Current Science,* November 11, 2011.

Kim Zetter, "How Digital Detectives Deciphered Stuxnet, the Most Menacing Malware in History," *Wired*, July 11, 2011.

Internet Sources

Richard Adhikari, "Pentagon Rattles Its Cyber-Saber," *TechNewsWorld*, March 29, 2012. www.technewsworld.com/story/Pentagon-Rattles -Its-Cyber-Saber-72880.html.

Stuart Fox, "Cyberwar: Definition, Hype and Reality," *Security News Daily*, July 2, 2011. www.securitynewsdaily.com/828-cyberwar-defi nition-cyber-war.html.

James Andrew Lewis, "Cyber Attacks, Real or Imagined, and Cyber War," Center for Strategic and International Studies, July 11, 2011. http:// csis.org/publication/cyber-attacks-real-or-imagined-and-cyber-war.

John P. Mello Jr., "Threat of Military Retaliation for Cyber Attacks May Be More Bluster than Brawn," *Government Security News*, June 1, 2011. www.gsnmagazine.com/article/23470/threat_military _retaliation_cyber_attacks_may_be_m.

Katitza Rodriquez, "The Impending Cybersecurity Power Grab— It's Not Just for the United States," Electronic Frontier Foundation, April 18, 2012. www.eff.org/deeplinks/2012/04/impending -cybersecurity-power-grab-its-not-just-united-states.

US Department of Defense, *Department of Defense Strategy for Operating in Cyberspace*, July 2011. www.defense.gov/news/d20110714cyber.pdf.

Source Notes

Overview

1. Ralph Langner, in Steve Kroft, "Stuxnet: Computer Worm Opens New Era of Warfare," *60 Minutes*, CBS News, March 4, 2012. www.cbsnews.com.
2. Robert M. Lee, "Stuxnet and the Paradigm Shift in Cyber Warfare," Control Global, May 19, 2011. www.controlglobal.com.
3. Richard A. Clarke and Robert K. Knake, *Cyber War: The Next Threat to National Security and What to Do About It*. New York: HarperCollins, 2010, p. 69.
4. Quoted in Homeland Security News Wire, "Defining Cyber Warfare," February 23, 2011. www.homelandsecuritynewswire.com.
5. Quoted in Stuart Fox, "Cyberwar: Definition, Hype and Reality," *Security News Daily*, July 2, 2011. www.securitynewsdaily.com.
6. Paul Rosenzweig, "From Worms to Cyber War," *Defining Ideas*, December 9, 2011. www.hoover.org.
7. Tony Bradley, "Zero Day Exploits," About.com Internet/Network Security. http://netsecurity.about.com.
8. Jeffrey Carr, "What Is Cyberwar?," *Slate*, August 12, 2011. www.slate.com.
9. Stewart Baker, Natalia Filipiak, and Katrina Timlin, *In the Dark*, McAfee/Center for Strategic and International Studies, 2011. www.mcafee.com.
10. Baker, Filipiak, and Timlin, *In the Dark*.
11. William L. Tafoya, "Cyber Terror," *FBI Law Enforcement Bulletin*, November 2011. www.fbi.gov.
12. Catherine A. Theohary and John Rollins, *Terrorist Use of the Internet: Information Operations in Cyberspace*, Congressional Research Service, March 8, 2011.
13. Lee, "Stuxnet and the Paradigm Shift in Cyber Warfare."
14. Quoted in Stuart Fox, "What Cyberwar Would Look Like," *Security News Daily*, July 2, 2011. www.securitynewsdaily.com.
15. Tafoya, "Cyber Terror."
16. Quoted in Matt Liebowitz and Paul Wagenseil, "Power Grids, Oil Refineries Face 'Staggering' Levels of Cyberattacks," *Security News Daily*, April 19, 2011. www.securitynewsdaily.com.
17. Quoted in Mark Clayton, "From the Man Who Discovered Stuxnet, Dire Warnings One Year Later," *Christian Science Monitor*, September 22, 2011. www.csmonitor.com.
18. Quoted in Clayton, "From the Man Who Discovered Stuxnet."
19. Quoted in Siobhan Gorman and Julian E. Barnes, "Cyber Combat: Act of War," *Wall Street Journal*, May 30, 2011. http://online.wsj.com.
20. Scott J. Shackelford and Richard B. Andres, "State Responsibility for Cyber Attacks: Competing Standards for a Growing Problem," *Georgetown Journal of International Law*, 2011. http://gjil.org.

What Is Cyberwarfare?

21. William J. Lynn III, "Defending a New Domain," *Foreign Affairs*, September/October 2010. www.foreignaffairs.com.
22. Lynn, "Defending a New Domain."
23. Quoted in William Pentland, "Still Recovering from Largest Cyber Attack on Record, U.S. Military Creates 'Cyber Unit,'" *Forbes*, July 24, 2011. www.forbes.com.
24. Dmitri Alperovitch, *Revealed: Opera-*

www.fas.org.

tion Shady RAT, McAfee, August 2011. www.mcafee.com.

25. Alperovitch, *Revealed: Operation Shady RAT*.

26. Clarke and Knake, *Cyber War: The Next Threat to National Security and What to Do About It*, p. 20.

27. Rob Rosenberger, "Media Lacks 'Thousands Feared Dead' Headlines in Russian-Georgian Cyber-War," *Vmyths*, August 18, 2008. http://vmyths.com.

28. Quoted in Kim Hart, "Longtime Battle Lines Are Recast in Russia and Georgia's Cyberwar," *Washington Post*, August 14, 2008. www.washingtonpost.com

29. Jeffrey Carr, *Inside Cyber Warfare: Mapping the Cyber Underworld*. Sebastopol, CA: O'Reilly Media, 2010, p. 13.

30. Phillip Porras, Hassen Saidi, and Vinod Yegneswaran, *Conficker C Analysis*, SRI International, March 4, 2009. http://mtc.sri.com.

31. Porras, Saidi, and Yegneswaran, *Conficker C Analysis*.

32. Ellen Nakashima, "Foreign Hackers Targeted U.S. Water Plant in Apparent Malicious Cyber Attack, Expert Says," *Washington Post*, November 18, 2011. www.washingtonpost.com.

33. Jim Ivers, comment on Brian Krebs, "Cyber Intrusion Blamed for Hardware Failure at Water Utility," *Krebs on Security* (blog), November 18, 2011. http://krebsonsecurity.com.

How Great a Threat Is Cyberwarfare?

34. Quoted in Eli Lake, "Outgoing FBI Cybercop Warns of a 'Grossly Underappreciated' Threat," *Daily Beast*, April 25, 2012. www.thedailybeast.com.

35. Shawn Henry, testimony before the House Homeland Security Subcommittee on Oversight, Investigations, and Management, April 24, 2012. http://homeland.house.gov.

36. Henry, testimony before the House Homeland Security Subcommittee on Oversight, Investigations, and Management.

37. Quoted in Matt Liebowitz and Paul Wagenseil, "Power Grids, Oil Refineries Face 'Staggering' Levels of Cyberattacks," *Security News Daily*, April 19, 2011. www.securitynewsdaily.com.

38. Baker, Filipiak, and Timlin, *In the Dark*.

39. pr0f, interview by Chester Wisniewski, "Interview with SCADA Hacker pr0f About the State of Infrastructure Security," *Naked Security*, November 22, 2011. http://nakedsecurity.sophos.com.

40. pr0f, "The Grid: A Digital Frontier," Pastebin, November 18, 2011. http://pastebin.com.

41. Environmental Defense Fund, "Smart Grid: Revolutionizing Our Energy Future," 2012. www.edf.org.

42. Henry, testimony before the House Homeland Security Subcommittee on Oversight, Investigations, and Management.

43. Baker, Filipiak, and Timlin, *In the Dark*.

44. Quoted in Siobhan Gorman, "Electricity Grid in U.S. Penetrated by Spies," *Wall Street Journal*, April 8, 2009.

45. Office of the National Counterintelligence Executive, *Foreign Spies Stealing US Economic Secrets in Cyberspace*, October 2011. www.ncix.gov.

46. Bruce Schneier, participant in "The Cyber War Threat Has Been Grossly Exaggerated" debate, Intelligence Squared, June 8, 2010. http://intelligencesquared us.org.

47. Jerry Brito and Tate Watkins, "Loving the Cyber Bomb? The Dangers of Threat Inflation in Cybersecurity Policy," Mercatus Center, April 2011. http://mercatus.org.

48. Brito and Watkins, "Loving the Cyber Bomb?"

What Is the Best Protection Against Cyberwarfare?

49. Quoted in Tom Gjelten, "Stuxnet Raises 'Blowback' Risk in Cyberwar," NPR, November 2, 2011. www.npr.org.

50. Gjelten, "Stuxnet Raises 'Blowback' Risk in Cyberwar."

51. Terry Benzel, in "Preventing a 'Cyber-Pearl Harbor,'" PBS, April 12, 2012. www.pbs.org.

52. Gordon M. Snow, "Statement Before the Senate Judiciary Committee, Subcommittee on Crime and Terrorism," Federal Bureau of Investigation, April 12, 2011. www.fbi.gov.

53. Baker, Filipiak, and Timlin, *In the Dark*.

54. Jim Dempsey, "Don't Mess with Success," Center for Democracy and Technology, June 17, 2011. www.cdt.org.

55. Dempsey, "Don't Mess with Success."

56. Quoted in RedOrbit, "Vote Nears on Controversial Cybersecurity Bill (CISPA)," April 19, 2012. www.redorbit.com.

57. Joseph I. Lieberman, opening statement for Senate hearing "Securing America's Future: The Cybersecurity Act of 2012," February 16, 2012. www.hsdl.org.

58. Robert Johnston, in "Public Power Confronts Change," *EnergyBiz*, September/October 2011. www.energybiz.com.

59. Quoted in Tom Gjelten, "Cybersecurity Bill: Vital Need or Just More Rules?," NPR, March 22, 2012. www.npr.org.

60. Henry, testimony before the House Homeland Security Subcommittee on Oversight, Investigations, and Management.

How Should Governments Respond to Cyberattacks?

61. Quoted in Eric Schmitt and Thom Shanker, "U.S. Debated Cyberwarfare in Attack Plan on Libya," *New York Times*, October 17, 2011. www.nytimes.com.

62. William J. Lynn III, "The Pentagon's Cyberstrategy, One Year Later," *Foreign Affairs*, September 28, 2011. www.foreignaffairs.com.

63. Eric Sterner, "Retaliatory Deterrence in Cyberspace," *Strategic Studies Quarterly*, Spring 2011. www.au.af.mil.

64. Nick Harvey, "Forget a Cyber Maginot Line," *Guardian*, May 30, 2011. www.guardian.co.uk.

65. Benjamin H. Friedman and Christopher Preble, "A Military Response to Cyberattacks Is Preposterous," Cato Institute, June 2, 2011. www.cato.org.

66. Friedman and Preble, "A Military Response to Cyberattacks Is Preposterous."

67. Quoted in John P. Mello Jr., "Threat of Military Retaliation for Cyber Attacks May Be More Bluster than Brawn," *Government Security News*, June 1, 2011. www.gsnmagazine.com.

68. Mike McConnell, Michael Chertoff, and William J. Lynn III, "China's Cyber Thievery Is National Policy—and Must Be Challenged," *Wall Street Journal*, January 27, 2012. http://online.wsj.com.

69. Quoted in Gorman, "Electricity Grid in U.S. Penetrated by Spies."

70. James Andrew Lewis, "Cyber Attacks, Real or Imagined, and Cyber War," Center for Strategic and International Studies, July 11, 2011. http://csis.org.

71. Sterner, "Retaliatory Deterrence in Cyberspace."

72. Quoted in Ellen Nakashima, "List of Cyber-Weapons Developed by Pentagon to Streamline Computer Warfare," *Washington Post*, May 31, 2011. www.washingtonpost.com.

List of Illustrations

Index

Note: numbers in bold indicate illustrations